20th THE Century Children's Poetry Treasury

selected by Jack Prelutsky

illustrated by Meilo So

Alfred A. Knopf  New York

For Susan Hirschman and Janet Schulman—
my wise and patient editors
and
For Carolynn Kim-Prelutsky—
my treasure

J.P.

To my old ink garden

M.S.

THIS IS A BORZOI BOOK PUBLISHED BY ALFRED A. KNOPF, INC.

Compilation copyright © 1999 by Jack Prelutsky. Illustrations copyright © 1999 by Meilo So.
Published in the United States by Alfred A. Knopf, Inc., New York, and simultaneously
in Canada by Random House of Canada Limited, Toronto.

Distributed by Random House, Inc., New York.

KNOPF, BORZOI BOOKS, and the colophon are registered trademarks of Random House, Inc.

Hand-lettering by Bernard Maisner.

Acknowledgments for permission to reprint previously published material appear on pages 91–94.

www.randomhouse.com/kids

Library of Congress Cataloging-in-Publication Data

The 20th-century children's poetry treasury / selected by Jack Prelutsky ; illustrated by Meilo So.

p.   cm.

Includes index.

SUMMARY: A collection of more than 200 poems by such modern poets as Nikki Grimes, John Ciardi, Karla Kuskin,
Ted Hughes, e. e. cummings, Eve Merriam, Deborah Chandra, Arnold Adoff, and more than 100 others.

ISBN 0-679-89314-8 (trade). — ISBN 0-679-99314-2 (lib. bdg.)

1. Children's poetry, American. 2. American poetry—20th century. 3. English poetry—20th century. 4. Children's poetry, English.
[1. American poetry—Collections. 2. English poetry—Collections.] I. Prelutsky, Jack. II. So, Meilo, ill.
III. Title: Twentieth-century children's poetry treasury.

PS586.3.T27   1999

811'.50809282—dc21   99-23988

Printed in the United States of America

10 9 8 7 6 5 4 3 2 1

September 1999

Introduction

Almost thirty-five years ago, when I wrote my first poems for children, I was unaware of the rich tradition I was embracing. I was unfamiliar with the work of most of my predecessors, and did not realize that I was following in their footsteps. In fact, my editor cautioned me about reading *any* children's poetry, fearing that my emerging voice might be unduly influenced. I followed her advice for about ten years, until we both felt sufficiently secure that I had developed my own style. Then, little by little, I began exploring the work of other children's poets. I was delighted by what I found, and soon was reading every bit of children's verse I could get my hands on. Reading led to collecting, and soon both became passions.

This treasury has been culled almost entirely from my private collection of children's poetry books, which I estimate now exceeds four thousand volumes. I read thousands of poems to select slightly over two hundred that I felt *represented* the scope and variety of children's verse produced in the twentieth century, and had no trouble including at least one poem from every decade. Children's literature in general has blossomed in our time, and poetry in particular has entered a "golden age."

Until this century, most children's poetry was either syrupy sweet or overblown and didactic, and tended to talk down to its readers. Contemporary children's poets have thrown all that condescension and moralizing out the window, and write with today's *real child* in mind. They write about sports, sibling rivalry, outer space, monsters, food fights, school, and just plain silliness. Of course today's poets still address the ageless themes of children's poetry—imagination, nature and the seasons, Who am I?, wordplay, and the many moods of human beings. My final selections represent all of these and many more.

I truly believe that most of the best poetry for children has been written during my own creative lifetime. With this in mind, this collection is weighted with the poetry of my contemporaries. I've also done my best to include a number of lesser-known poets, as well as poets who began publishing after the appearance of my first anthology, *The Random House Book of Poetry for Children*, in 1983.

I would be remiss if I didn't mention that there *were* some notable exceptions to the "children should be seen and not heard" school of writing. These include Lewis Carroll, Edward Lear, Hilaire Belloc, Eugene Field, and Robert Louis Stevenson. In fact, we often think of them as twentieth-century writers, but they produced their work in the nineteenth century. Therefore, I was unable to include them in this volume.

Children's poets today are producing some wonderful work, and it's apparent to me that the torch is being passed to very capable hands. The renaissance continues into the twenty-first century, and I am delighted.

—*Jack Prelutsky*
Mercer Island, Washington, September 1999

Magic Landscape

Shall I draw a magic landscape?
In the genius of my fingers
I hold the seeds.
Can I grow a painting like a flower?
Can I sculpture a future without weeds?

—*Joyce Carol Thomas*

Genius

"Sis! Wake up!" I whisper
in the middle of the night.

Urgently, I shake her
till she switches on the light.

The spiral notebook in my hand
provides her quick relief.

It tells her there's no danger
of a break-in by a thief.

"Okay," she says, then, props herself
up vertically in bed.

She nods for me to read my work.
I cough, then forge ahead.

The last verse of my poem leaves
her silent as a mouse.

I worry till she says, "We have
a genius in the house."

—*Nikki Grimes*

2

Spells

I need no spell to get me through
A tangled fence of briars.
I need no spell to help me pass
A wall of burning fires.

I need no spell to make a dress
Of silk from one of chintz.
I need no spell to turn a frog
Into a handsome prince.

But if you've got a spell around
That gets my homework right,
Or one that makes my mother think
I've gone to bed at night,

Or one that takes the garbage out,
Or one that feeds the cat,
I'd pay you my allowance
If you had a spell like that!

—Jane Yolen

Magic

Sandra's seen a leprechaun,
Eddie touched a troll,
Laurie danced with witches once,
Charlie found some goblins' gold.
Donald heard a mermaid sing,
Susy spied an elf,
But all the magic I have known
I've had to make myself.

—Shel Silverstein

3

The Sidewalk Racer
Or
On the Skateboard

Skimming
an asphalt sea
I swerve, I curve, I
sway; I speed to whirring
sound an inch above the
ground; I'm the sailor
and the sail, I'm the
driver and the wheel
I'm the one and only
single engine
human auto
mobile.

—*Lillian Morrison*

Learning

I'm learning to say thank you.
And I'm learning to say please.
And I'm learning to use Kleenex,
Not my sweater, when I sneeze.
And I'm learning not to dribble.
And I'm learning not to slurp.
And I'm learning (though it sometimes
    really hurts me)
Not to burp.
And I'm learning to chew softer
When I eat corn on the cob.
And I'm learning that it's much
Much easier to be a slob.

—*Judith Viorst*

A Circle of Sun

I'm dancing.
I'm leaping.
I'm skipping about.
I gallop.
I grin.
I giggle.
I shout.
I'm Earth's many colors.
I'm morning and night.
I'm honey on toast.
I'm funny.
I'm bright.
I'm swinging.
I'm singing.
I wiggle.
I run.
I'm a piece of the sky
In a circle of sun.

—*Rebecca Kai Dotlich*

Running Song

I am running,
running, running.
I am running
just for fun.
Through the grass
and through the gravel
running faster
see me travel
past the people
staring, staring.
They are thinking
something's wrong.
I'm not looking.
I'm not caring.
I'm just running
hard and long.

Now my feet are
pounding pavement.
Now my heart is
pounding, too.
I can feel the sidewalk searing
through the bottom of my shoe.
How the wind is
whipping past me.
How the trees are
whizzing by.
Rushing rivers
run forever.
Maybe I can
if I try.

—*Marci Ridlon*

My Name Is...

My name is Sluggery-wuggery
My name is Worms-for-tea
My name is Swallow-the-table-leg
My name is Drink-the-Sea.

My name is I-eat-saucepans
My name is I-like-snails
My name is Grand-piano-George
My name is I-ride-whales.

My name is Jump-the-chimney
My name is Bite-my-knee
My name is Jiggery-pokery
And Riddle-me-ree, and ME.

—*Pauline Clarke*

Me

"My nose is blue,
My teeth are green,
My face is like a soup tureen.
I look just like a lima bean.
I'm very, very lovely.
My feet are far too short
And long.
My hands are left and right
And wrong.
My voice is like the hippo's song.
I'm very, very,
Very, very,
Very, very
Lovely?"

—*Karla Kuskin*

Mosquito

There is more
To a mosquito
Than her sting
Or the way she sings
In the ear:

There are her wings
As clear
As windows,
There are the sleek
Velvets on her back;

She bends six
Slender knees,
And her eye, that
Sees the swatter,
Glitters.

—*Valerie Worth*

Butterfly Cloth

How fragile
Floats the butterfly,
A banner barely cloth.
Woven of sterner stuff
It seems,
The tapestry of moth.

—*Victoria Forrester*

Dragonfly

This sky-ballerina,
this glimmering
jewel,
glides in a gown
of lucid blue—
with wings that you
could *whisper* through.

—*Rebecca Kai Dotlich*

Blue-Butterfly Day

It is blue-butterfly day here in spring,
And with these sky-flakes down in flurry on flurry
There is more unmixed color on the wing
Than flowers will show for days unless they hurry.

But these are flowers that fly and all but sing:
And now from having ridden out desire
They lie closed over in the wind and cling
Where wheels have freshly sliced the April mire.

—*Robert Frost*

6

Ants, Although Admirable, Are Awfully Aggravating

The busy ant works hard all day
And never stops to rest or play.
He carries things ten times his size,
And never grumbles, whines or cries.
And even climbing flower stalks,
He always runs, he never walks.
He loves his work, he never tires,
And never puffs, pants or perspires.

Yet though I praise his boundless vim
I am not really fond of him.

— *Walter R. Brooks*

Cricket

A metal bug
with rusty tongue,
and throat stuck shut.

The song he makes
comes chiseled off,
small scrapes,
tin flakes.

His voice opens,
closes,
on a hinge.
A metal self
is all he's got.
He stops.

Winds a spring,
kicks stiff bolts,
then on he sings
with raspy bits of
rusted things.

— *Deborah Chandra*

Beetles

Beetles must use polish,
    They look so new and shiny,
Just like a freshly painted car,
    Except for being tiny.

— *Monica Shannon*

The Centipede

I objurgate the centipede,
A bug we do not really need.
At sleepy-time he beats a path
Straight to the bedroom or the bath.
You always wallop where he's not,
Or, if he is, he makes a spot.

— *Ogden Nash*

Doris Skips

Doris skips,
    Dolores prances,
Delia scurries,
    Della dances,
Daphne walks
    With queenly grace,
Dolly always
    Wins the race,
Darcy marches,
    Donna ambles,
Dorothy lopes,
    And Dora scrambles.
Almost every
    Girl you meet
Has some special way
    With feet.

—*Leland B. Jacobs*

What Is the Opposite of Hat?

What is the opposite of *hat*?
It isn't hard to answer that.
It's *shoes*, for shoes and hat together
Protect our two extremes from weather.

Between these two extremes there lies
A middle, which you would be wise
To clothe as well, or you'll be chilly
And run the risk of looking silly.

—*Richard Wilbur*

The Gentle Cow

The gentle cow is good and kind.
All day she chews with quiet mind.
She eats and eats the green, green grass,
And then I drink it in a glass.

—*Mary Morris Duane*

The Lizard

The Time to Tickle a Lizard,
Is Before, or Right After, a Blizzard.
Now the place to begin
Is just under his Chin—
And here's more Advice:
Don't Poke more than Twice
At an Intimate Place like his Gizzard.

—*Theodore Roethke*

The Crocodile

This is a Crocodile, my boy…
Or is it an Alligator?…
I've an excellent book that you'll enjoy
We can refer to later;

The Alligator…no, Crocodile
Is a purplish colour beneath.
Give it a tickle to make it smile
And let's count the number of teeth,

For the Croc. (I think) has a row too few
Though the 'Gator can't wink its eye…

Ah!
      Now I can tell you which of the two
You have just been eaten by.

—*Michael Flanders*

Tent

My skin is like
A canvas tent
That's stretched
From bone to bone;
It's cut to measure
Just for me,
I wonder where
It's sewn?
And why can't I
Unzip the front
And roam outside,
Then in?
But here I stay
Each night, each day,
Alone,
Within my skin.

—*Deborah Chandra*

At the Bottom of the Garden

No, it isn't an old football
grown all shrunken and prickly
because it was left out so long
at the bottom of the garden.

It's only Hedgehog
who, when she thinks I'm not looking,
unballs herself to move…
Like bristling black lightning.

—*Grace Nichols*

9

December Leaves

The fallen leaves are cornflakes
That fill the lawn's wide dish,
And night and noon
The wind's a spoon
That stirs them with a swish.

The sky's a silver sifter,
A-sifting white and slow,
That gently shakes
On crisp brown flakes
The sugar known as snow.

—*Kaye Starbird*

The Snowflake

Before I melt,
Come look at me!
This lovely icy filigree!
Of a great forest
In one night
I make a wilderness
Of white:
By skyey cold
Of crystals made,
All softly, on
Your finger laid,
I pause, that you
My beauty see:
Breathe, and I vanish
Instantly.

—*Walter de la Mare*

The More It Snows

The more it
SNOWS-tiddely-pom,
The more it
GOES-tiddely-pom
The more it
GOES-tiddely-pom
On
Snowing.

And nobody
KNOWS-tiddely-pom,
How cold my
TOES-tiddely-pom
How cold my
TOES-tiddely-pom
Are
Growing.

—A. A. Milne

White Cat Winter

White cat Winter
prowls
the farm,
tiptoes
soft
through withered corn,
creeps
along low walls
of stone,
falls asleep
beside
the barn.

—Tony Johnston

11

Where Are You Now?

When the night begins to fall
And the sky begins to glow
You look up and see the tall
City of light begin to grow—
In rows and little golden squares
The lights come out. First here, then there
Behind the windowpanes as though
A million billion bees had built
Their golden hives and honeycombs
Above you in the air.

—*Mary Britton Miller*

The Moon's the North Wind's Cooky

The Moon's the North Wind's cooky.
He bites it, day by day,
Until there's but a rim of scraps
That crumble all away.

The South Wind is a baker.
He kneads clouds in his den,
And bakes a crisp new moon *that…greedy
North…Wind…eats…again!*

—*Vachel Lindsay*

Summer Stars

Bend low again, night of summer stars.
So near you are, sky of summer stars,
So near, a long-arm man can pick off stars,
Pick off what he wants in the sky bowl,
So near you are, summer stars,
So near, strumming, strumming,
    So lazy and hum-strumming.

—Carl Sandburg

Fireflies

An August night—
    The wind not quite
A wind, the sky
    Not just a sky—
And everywhere
    The speckled air
Of summer stars
    Alive in jars.

—J. Patrick Lewis

My Window Screen

My window screen, all crisscrossed wire,
Has half a million eyes,
Each big enough to let in air
But baffle summer flies.

Mosquito comes, he bumps his head—
My screen won't open wide.
All night it strains between my bed
And all there is outside.

—X. J. Kennedy

13

The Noise of Nothing

The noise of nothing
is less than a pin
petering down
a deep apple bin,

less than a bubble,
blown round and ripe,
sliding up
off the brim of a pipe,

less than the ring
of a rain-drop gone
from the pool it tingled
and circled on,

less than a penny
put down in plush,
less than a web
where moth-wings hush,

less than a dew
the size of a drop,
drying by noon
on a petal's lip,

less than the hiss
if starlight fell
down the abyss
of a bottomless well,

less than something,
least of the small:
the noise of nothing's
no sound at all.

Has anyone heard it
breathe or blow?
ripple or stir?
No one I know.

—*Norma Farber*

Night Sounds

In the street
       sounds of wheels humming,
       sounds of heels drumming.
Humming and drumming,
Keeping me from sleeping.
In the house
       sounds of words mumbling,
       overheard grumbling.
Mumbling and grumbling,
Keeping me unsleeping.
Far away
       sounds of waves lashing,
       quietly crashing.
Lashing and crashing,
Sweeping me to sleep.

—*Felice Holman*

Sound

There is a chatter in the barnyard,
There are wind, and bee, and bird;
In the middle of the silence
The country sounds are heard.

While sometimes in the city
With noises all around,
There will be a little quiet
In the very midst of sound.

—*Anna Bird Stewart*

14

Ears Hear

Flies buzz,
Motors roar.
Kettles hiss,
People snore.
Dogs bark,
Birds cheep.
Autos honk: *Beep! Beep!*

Winds sigh,
Shoes squeak.
Trucks honk,
Floors creak.
Whistles toot,
Bells clang.
Doors slam: *Bang! Bang!*

Kids shout,
Clocks ding.
Babies cry,
Phones ring.
Balls bounce,
Spoons drop.
People scream: *Stop! Stop!*

—*Lucia M. and James L. Hymes Jr.*

The Nightnoise Gladiator

When the radiator hisses,
when the hall stairs creak and moan,
when there's something downstairs ringing
but it's not the telephone;

When the back door lock is squeaking,
when you think you hear a knock,
when there's something upstairs ticking
and it's not Grandfather's clock;

When the refrigerator rattles,
when the window curtains swish,
when the bathroom sink *drip-drips, drip-drips,*
I close my eyes and wish

I had a Nightnoise Gladiator.
There is nothing he enjoys
more than eating till he's gobbled up
his enemy: Night Noise.

—*Richard Michelson*

15

Tuning Up

I'm at a concert
And the tuba moans.
The tuba moans
And the bassoon groans.
The bassoon groans
And the violin sings.
The violin sings
And the cymbal rings.
The cymbal rings
And the trumpet toots.
The trumpet toots
And the flutist flutes.
The flutist flutes
And the drummer drums.
The drummer drums
And the cello hums....
Then ending all this dissonance
The baton raps and starts to dance.

—Felice Holman

My Violin

My mom brought home a violin
so I could learn to play.
She told me if I practiced hard
I'd play it well someday.

Without a single lesson,
I tried to play a song.
My fiddle squeaked, my fiddle squawked.
The notes came out all wrong.

My little brother fled the room.
Mom covered up her ears.
My puppy dog began to howl.
My sister was in tears.

My dad pulled out his wallet.
He handed me a ten.
He made me swear I'd never play
that violin again.

—Bruce Lansky

The Girl Who Makes the Cymbals Bang

I'm the girl who makes the cymbals bang—
It used to be a boy
That got to play them in the past
Which always would annoy

Me quite a bit. Though I complained,
Our teacher Mister Cash
Said, "Sorry, girls don't have the strength
To come up with a crash."

"Oh yeah?" said I. "Please give them here!"
And there and then, I slammed
Together those brass plates so hard
His eardrums traffic-jammed.

He gulped and gaped, and I could tell
His old ideas were bending—
So now me and my cymbals give
Each song a real smash ending.

—X. J. Kennedy

Music Class

I hear birds. I sing frogs.
My heart hears every note,
yet my song is locked
inside my throat.
Someone laughs.
I'm way off-key.

The teacher holds my hand
and opens a special box
of things with secret voices.
I get maracas and triangle.
I am aria. I am madrigal.
With silver bells and tambourine,
I can sing!

—Kristine O'Connell George

17

The Hawk

I stare
       I glare
I gaze
       I gawk
With keen
Mean eyes
I am the hawk.
All day I pray
For prey to view.
Be thankful if
I don't
See
YOU!

—Douglas Florian

Hawk in the Tree

One look at Hawk's
stern face,
the fierce hooked beak,
the motionless shape
in the crook of a tree,
keen and sharp and sure,

and I am
shoulder to shoulder
with the mouse,

I feel the squirrel's
fear,

even the snake's
cold blood
turning colder.

—Constance Levy

Advice for a Frog
(Concerning a Crane)

Watch out, Old Croaker.
Here comes Stick Walker,
here comes Pond Poker,
here comes Death.

Take a breath, Slick Skin.
Muck down, sink in.
Don't make bubbles.
Good luck, Grin Chin—

here comes Trouble.

—Alice Schertle

18

Wolf

As soon as you say this word
snow begins to fall

W O L F

A shadow-word   undefined
as fog   it slips behind
sketches of dark pines
and birch trunks
its footprints quick
on the snowy page

W O L F

Whenever you say this word
a little girl fastens her red
cloak   and hurries along
the path

Muzzle turned
to the north wind
W O L F   runs
through the penciled woods
a winter moon
caught in its eyes

—*Barbara Juster Esbensen*

Orang-utan

Watch me,
touch me,
catch-me-if-you-can!
I am
soundless,
swung-from-your-sight,
gone with the wind,
shiver of air,
trick-of-the-light.

Watch me,
touch me,
catch-me-if-you-dare!
I hide, I glide,
I stride through air,
shatter the day-star dappled light
over forest floor.
The world's in my grasp!
I am windsong,
sky-flier,
man-of-the-woods,
the arm of the law.

—*Judith Nicholls*

19

For Sale

One sister for sale!
One sister for sale!
One crying and spying young sister for sale!
I'm really not kidding,
So who'll start the bidding?
Do I hear a dollar?
A nickel?
A penny?
Oh, isn't there, isn't there, isn't there any
One kid who will buy this old sister for sale,
This crying and spying young sister for sale?

—*Shel Silverstein*

Big Sister

I have a big sister;
She's taller and older;
On tiptoe I only
Reach up to her shoulder;
But I have a secret
That I haven't told her.
    (It's how to grow faster
    Until I grow past her.)

I watch what she's eating;
I watch what she's drinking;
I don't let her notice
Or see what I'm thinking;
But each time that she
Takes a bite, I take two;
And that way she only
Eats half what I do.

I have a big sister;
She's taller and older;
On tiptoe I only
Reach up to her shoulder;
But I have a secret
That I haven't told her.
(The way I will beat her
Is just to outeat her!)

—*Mary Ann Hoberman*

Rules

Do not jump on ancient uncles.
*
Do not yell at average mice.
*
Do not wear a broom to breakfast.
*
Do not ask a snake's advice.
*
Do not bathe in chocolate pudding.
*
Do not talk to bearded bears.
*
Do not smoke cigars on sofas.
*
Do not dance on velvet chairs.
*
Do not take a whale to visit
Russell's mother's cousin's yacht.
*
And whatever else you do do
It is better you
Do not.

—*Karla Kuskin*

Tickle Tickle

me papa tickle me feet
he call it "finger treat"
me scream and run each time he come
me papa tickle me feet

he tickle me tummy, me chest, me arm
his fingers fly so wild
he say, "Come here, little man.
You my ticklin' chile."

me papa say he love me
me papa look so proud
he say, "Sonny, what a joy
to see you laugh out loud."

he tickle me ribs, me neck, me back
his fingers grow longer each day
me twist and swing and laugh and kick
but he hold me anyway

me eyes, they water
me throat be sore
me weak, me dizzy
but me want more

he throw me high up in the air
and catch me from behind
me say, "Go higher!" and he say,
"Don't you know you're mine?"

me papa tickle me feet
he call it "finger treat"
me scream and run (but OH, WHAT FUN!)
when papa tickle me feet.

—*Dakari Hru*

21

Breakfast

I C U 8 your scrambled X,
I C U drank your T.
My heart is filled with NV,
R there NE X 4 me?
O Y is the carton MT now?
How greedy can U B?
4 U 8 all the scrambled X
And left me 1 green P!

— *Jeff Moss*

Tutti Frutti Lovesong

You are my darling CUMQUAT,
Oh, you're my PEACHy pie,
I think you are the BERRIES,
The APPLE of my eye.

Don't make me MELON-choly,
Please be my HONEY DEW,
'Cause oh, my sweet PAPAYA,
I'm BANANAS over you!

I would be oh, so GRAPEful
If you'd just say you care,
For it takes two to MANGO,
And we're a PEACHy PEAR.

Oh, ORANGE you a little
COCONUTS for me too?
Please say you'll be mon CHERRY,
I'm so GUAVA over you.

— *Mary Grace Dembeck*

We're Fearless Flying Hotdogs

We're fearless flying hotdogs,
the famous "Unflappable Five,"
we're mustered in formation
to climb, to dip, to dive,
we spread our wings with relish,
then reach for altitude,
we're aerobatic wieners,
the fastest flying food.

We're fearless flying hotdogs,
we race with flair and style,
then catch up with each other
and soar in single file,
you never saw such daring,
such power and control,
as when we swoop and spiral,
then slide into a roll.

The throngs applaud our antics,
they cheer us long and loud,
there's never a chilly reception,
there's never a sour crowd,
and if we may speak frankly,
we are a thrilling sight,
we're fearless flying hotdogs,
the delicate essence of flight.

—*Jack Prelutsky*

23

Spring

I'm shouting
I'm singing
I'm swinging through trees
I'm winging sky-high
With the buzzing black bees.
I'm the sun
I'm the moon
I'm the dew on the rose.
I'm a rabbit
Whose habit
Is twitching his nose.
I'm lively
I'm lovely
I'm kicking my heels.
I'm crying "Come dance"
To the freshwater eels.
I'm racing through meadows
Without any coat
I'm a gamboling lamb
I'm a light leaping goat
I'm a bud
I'm a bloom
I'm a dove on the wing.
I'm running on rooftops
And welcoming spring!

—*Karla Kuskin*

March

The sun is nervous
  As a kite
That can't quite keep
  Its own string tight.

Some days are fair,
  And some are raw.
The timid earth
  Decides to thaw.

Shy budlets peep
  From twigs on trees,
And robins join
  The chickadees.

Pale crocuses
  Poke through the ground
Like noses come
  To sniff around.

The mud smells happy
  On our shoes.
We still wear mittens,
  Which we lose.

—*John Updike*

24

april is a dog's dream

april is a dog's dream
the soft grass is growing
the sweet breeze is blowing
the air all full of singing feels just right
so no excuses now
we're going to the park
to chase and charge and chew
and I will make you see
what spring is all about

—*Marilyn Singer*

That May Morning

That May morning—very early—
As I walked the city street,
Not a single store was open
Any customer to greet.

That May morning—it was early—
As I walked the avenue,
I could stop and stare and window-shop,
And hear the pigeons coo.

Early, early that May morning
I could skip and jump and run
And make shadows on the sidewalk,
Not disturbing anyone.

All the windows, all the lamp posts,
Every leaf on every tree
That was growing through the sidewalk
Seemed to be there just for me.

—*Leland B. Jacobs*

25

Balloons

Such swollen creatures,
Holding their breath
While they swim
Dreamily from
Room to room.

Swaying slightly,
They wander the air-wisps,
Bumping and rubbing along the walls
Until they feel their fat backs
Bob against the ceiling.

Wanting nothing,
They drift and sleep—
Bald as babies,
Smooth moons of blue and red,
Nodding drowsy, spellbound heads.

—Deborah Chandra

Bubble

I made my lips grow
close and round,
and blew
into a plastic wand.
Then I saw it,
clear and thin—
my breath
wrapped in a
quivering skin
of soap that held
the blue of sky,
the sudden flash
of fireflies.
It made a trembling
shadow there,
slid whispering
through empty air,
to dip and soar
while full of glow,
I was surprised,
I didn't know
my own breath
could be a thing
so marble-round,
and glistening.

—Deborah Chandra

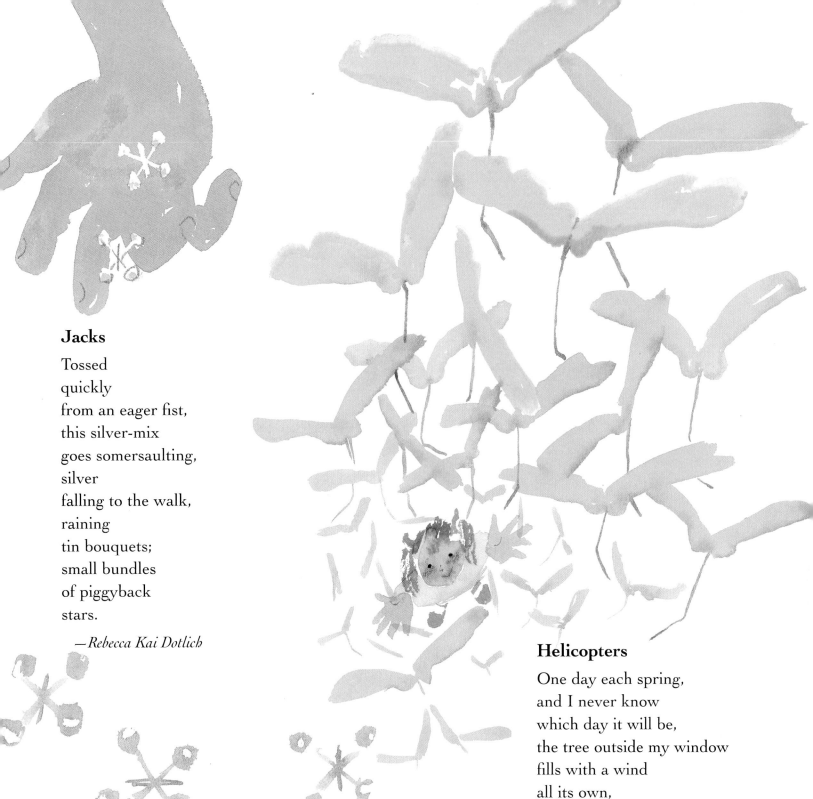

Jacks

Tossed
quickly
from an eager fist,
this silver-mix
goes somersaulting,
silver
falling to the walk,
raining
tin bouquets;
small bundles
of piggyback
stars.

—*Rebecca Kai Dotlich*

Helicopters

One day each spring,
and I never know
which day it will be,
the tree outside my window
fills with a wind
all its own,
swells like a giant
silk parasol,
lets fall
a wondrous storm
of helicopters,
pale, pale green.

—*Sylvia Cassedy*

27

Weather

Dot a dot dot   dot a dot dot
Spotting the windowpane.
Spack a spack speck   flick a flack fleck
Freckling the windowpane.

A spatter a scatter   a wet cat a clatter
A splatter a rumble outside.
Umbrella umbrella umbrella umbrella
Bumbershoot barrel of rain.

Slosh a galosh   slosh a galosh
Slither and slather and glide
A puddle a jump a puddle a jump
A puddle a jump puddle splosh
A juddle a pump aluddle a dump a
Puddmuddle jump in and slide!

                —*Eve Merriam*

Rain Sizes

Rain comes in various sizes.
Some rain is as small as a mist.
It tickles your face with surprises,
And tingles as if you'd been kissed.

Some rain is the size of a sprinkle
And doesn't put out all the sun.
You can see the drops sparkle and twinkle,
And a rainbow comes out when it's done.

Some rain is as big as a nickel
And comes with a crash and a hiss.
It comes down too heavy to tickle.
It's more like a splash than a kiss.

When it rains the right size and you're wrapped in
Your rainclothes, it's fun out of doors.
But run home before you get trapped in
The big rain that rattles and roars.

                —*John Ciardi*

Rain Sound

At first it's like drumming
as it patters down, then stops.
Now it's an animal
outside the window
quietly licking its chops.

—*Lillian Morrison*

April Rain Song

Let the rain kiss you.
Let the rain beat upon your head with silver
    liquid drops.
Let the rain sing you a lullaby.

The rain makes still pools on the sidewalk.
The rain makes running pools in the gutter.
The rain plays a little sleep-song on our roof at
    night—

And I love the rain.

—*Langston Hughes*

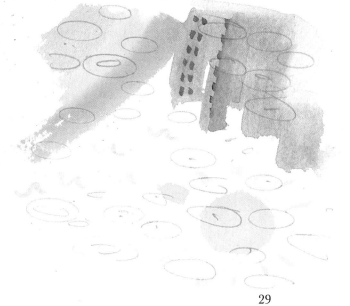

Wind Pictures

Look! There's a giant stretching in the sky,
A thousand white-maned horses flying by,
A house, a mother mountain with her hills,
A lazy lady posing in her frills,
Cotton floating from a thousand bales,
And a white ship with white sails.

See the old witch fumbling with her shawl,
White towers piling on a castle wall,
The bits of soft that break and fall away,
Air-borne mushrooms with undersides of gray—
Above, a white doe races with her fawn
On the white grass of a celestial lawn.
Lift up your lovely heads and look
As wind turns clouds into a picture book.

—*Mary O'Neill*

Sunflakes

If sunlight fell like snowflakes,
gleaming yellow and so bright,
we could build a sunman,
we could have a sunball fight,
we could watch the sunflakes
drifting in the sky.
We could go sleighing
in the middle of July
through sundrifts and sunbanks,
we could ride a sunmobile,
and we could touch sunflakes—
I wonder how they'd feel.

—*Frank Asch*

If Only

If I could be a grunting pig,
I would, and with my snout I'd dig
Deep down into the muddy ground
And deeper still until I found
A big potato, fat and sweet,
And then I'd eat and eat and eat
And when I'd eaten every bit
I'd fall asleep and dream of it:
That big potato, fat and round,
Deep down beneath the muddy ground.
Oh, with my snout I'd dig and dig…
If only I could be a pig.

—*Richard Edwards*

The Dream Keeper

Bring me all of your dreams,
You dreamers,
Bring me all of your
Heart melodies
That I may wrap them
In a blue cloud-cloth
Away from the too-rough fingers
Of the world.

—Langston Hughes

Oh, to Be…

"Oh, to be an eagle
And to swoop down from a peak
With the golden sunlight flashing
From the fierce hook of my beak.

"Oh, to be an eagle
And to terrify the sky
With a beat of wings like thunder
And a wild, barbaric cry.

"Oh…But why keep dreaming?
I must learn to be myself,"
Said the rubber duckling sadly
On its soapy bathroom shelf.

—Richard Edwards

I Can Fly

I can fly, of course,
Very low,
Not fast,
Rather slow.
I spread my arms
Like wings,
Lean on the wind,
And my body zings
About.
Nothing showy—
A few loops
And turns—
But for the most
Part,
I just coast.

However,
Since people are prone
To talk about
It,
I generally prefer,
Unless I am alone,
Just to walk about.

—Felice Holman

31

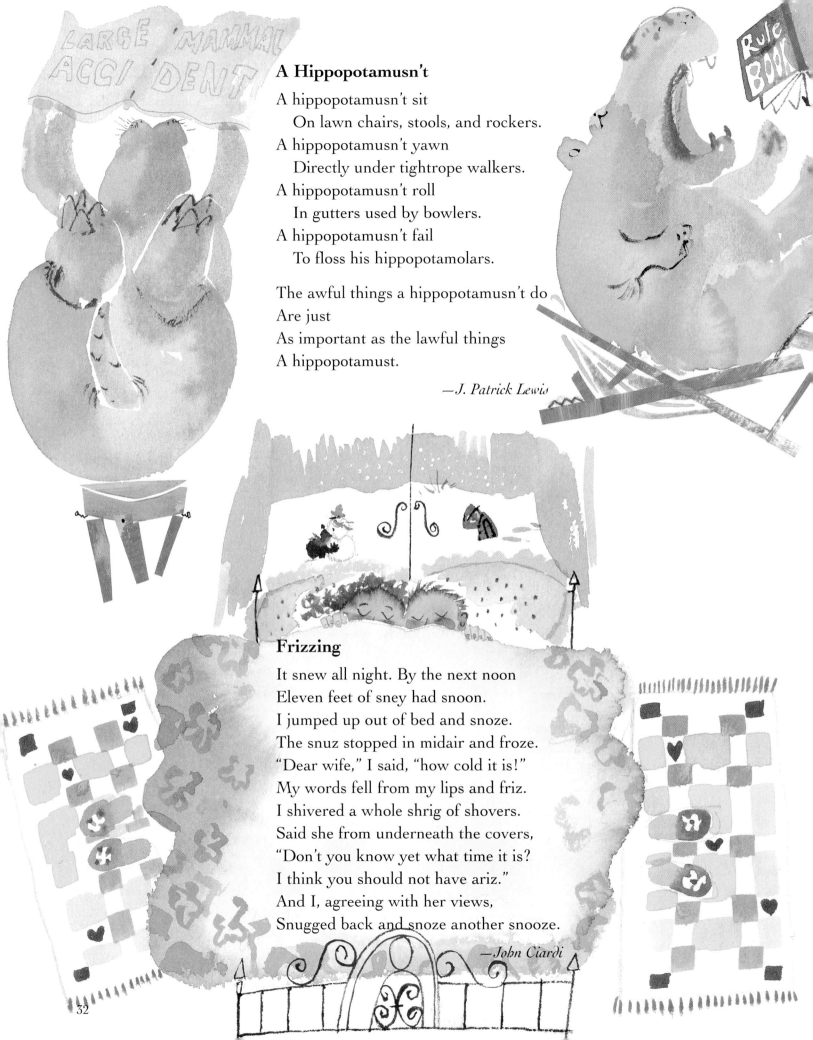

A Hippopotamusn't

A hippopotamusn't sit
  On lawn chairs, stools, and rockers.
A hippopotamusn't yawn
  Directly under tightrope walkers.
A hippopotamusn't roll
  In gutters used by bowlers.
A hippopotamusn't fail
  To floss his hippopotamolars.

The awful things a hippopotamusn't do
Are just
As important as the lawful things
A hippopotamust.

—J. Patrick Lewis

Frizzing

It snew all night. By the next noon
Eleven feet of sney had snoon.
I jumped up out of bed and snoze.
The snuz stopped in midair and froze.
"Dear wife," I said, "how cold it is!"
My words fell from my lips and friz.
I shivered a whole shrig of shovers.
Said she from underneath the covers,
"Don't you know yet what time it is?
I think you should not have ariz."
And I, agreeing with her views,
Snugged back and snoze another snooze.

—John Ciardi

The Sniffle

In spite of her sniffle,
Isabel's chiffle.
Some girls with a sniffle
Would be weepy and tiffle;
They would look awful,
Like a rained-on waffle,
But Isabel's chiffle
In spite of her sniffle.
Her nose is more red
With a cold in her head,
But then, to be sure,
Her eyes are bluer.
Some girls with a snuffle,
Their tempers are uffle,
But when Isabel's snivelly
She's snivelly civilly,
And when she is snuffly
She's perfectly luffly.

—Ogden Nash

The Click Clacker Machine

The Click Clacker Machine
    makes clackers that click.
The clackers click quickly
    but sometimes they stick.
When quick clicking clackers
    are sticking, they crack.
Then the clackers are clickless
    and put in a sack.
Sacked clackers are sent
    to the clicking inspectors
Who all claim to be
    clickless clacker collectors.

—Donna Lugg Pape

33

Vrooms

On a world near the sun live two brothers called VROOMS
Who, strangely enough, are built sort of like brooms
And they're stuck all alone up there high in the blue
And so, to kill time, just for something to do
Each one of these fellows takes turns with the other
In sweeping the dust off his world with his brother.

—*Dr. Seuss*

Loose and Limber

Loose and limber,
Beanbag Jim
Seems to have
No bones in him.
At carnivals
And vaudeville shows
He ties himself
In knots and bows.
He's known to all
Throughout the land
As nature's living
rubber band.

—*Arnold Lobel*

Stanley the Fierce

Stanley the Fierce
Has a chipped front tooth
And clumps of spiky hair.
And his hands are curled into
    two fat fists
And his arms are bulgy and bare.
And his smile is a tight little
    mean little smile
And his eyes give a shivery glare.
And I hear that he goes for seventeen days
Without changing his underwear.

But I don't think I'll ask him.

          —Judith Viorst

The People Upstairs

The people upstairs all practice ballet.
Their living room is a bowling alley.
Their bedroom is full of conducted tours.
Their radio is louder than yours.
They celebrate weekends all the week.
When they take a shower, your ceilings leak.
They try to get their parties to mix
By supplying their guests with Pogo sticks,
And when their orgy at last abates,
They go to the bathroom on roller skates.
I might love the people upstairs wondrous
If instead of above us, they just lived under us.

          —Ogden Nash

Tired Tim

Poor tired Tim! It's sad for him.
He lags the long bright morning through,
Ever so tired of nothing to do;
He moons and mopes the livelong day,
Nothing to think about, nothing to say;
Up to bed with his candle to creep,
Too tired to yawn, too tired to sleep:
Poor tired Tim! It's sad for him.

          —Walter de la Mare

Humming Birds

I think it is a funny thing
That some birds whistle, others sing.
The Warbler warbles in his throat,
The Sparrow only knows one note;
But he is better off than some,
For Humming Birds can only hum.

—Betty Sage

The Nest

Her day's just begun—
the ruby-throated hummingbird
drinks from the blue funnel
of the morning glory.
Then, from her dream
she builds;
her nest
a spider's
abandoned web,
emerald green mosses,
pale blue-green lichen,
mud,
leafmold—
offerings
from the living world.

Spirits of ancestors
hover nearby,
spirits that speak from the dream,
guiding her, showing the way.

With movements more rapid
than the human heart can beat,
she makes a cup
for the flurry
of other wings,
for the cool,
quicksilver
light
each blessed
morning
brings.

—Mary Ann Coleman

36

Red-Winged Blackbird

Red-winged blackbird takes the air
Very spruce and debonnaire,
And he flaunts to all beholders
Scarlet feathers on his shoulders.

—*Grace Taber Hallock*

No Shop Does the Bird Use

No shop does the bird use,
no counter nor baker,
but the bush is his orchard,
the grass is his acre,
the ant is his quarry,
the seed is his bread,
and a star is his candle
to light him to bed.

—*Elizabeth Coatsworth*

Woodpecker

Woodpecker is rubber-necked
    But has a nose of steel.
He bangs his head against the wall
    And cannot even feel.

When Woodpecker's jack-hammer head
    Starts up its dreadful din
Knocking the dead bough double dead
    How do his eyes stay in?

Pity the poor dead oak that cries
    In terrors and in pains.
But pity more Woodpecker's eyes
    And bouncing rubber brains.

—*Ted Hughes*

37

Fog

The fog comes
on little cat feet.

It sits looking
over harbor and city
on silent haunches
and then moves on.

— *Carl Sandburg*

Monopoly

From the hilltop you can see
the city, like Monopoly,
laid out on a paper board.

Little pieces far below,
plastic houses row on row,
holding little plastic folk
asking how the game is scored.

Little unseen plastic folk
driving through the city smoke,
following the boulevards,
taking chances,
taking cards,
driving all across the board
asking how the game is scored.

Little busy businesses
laid out on the streets below,
waiting for the plastic folk
driving through the city smoke,
driving cars with little wheels,
moving forward, making deals:
Boardwalk,
Park Place,
passing Go,
Reading Railroad,
B & O,

moving all across the board
asking how the game is scored.

— *Alice Schertle*

Pigeons

Other birds soar in the clouds

these are city dwellers
they see the sky
only between clumps of buildings

they nest on fire escapes
air conditioners
basement stoops

they can nest on nails

they are gray and bedraggled
they flap their wings in the midst of filth
and they make more filth

they are noisy
they are disgusting
they have an iridescent beauty

they huddle   they survive

—*Eve Merriam*

Sidewalks

A sidewalk is a wide walk
  A let's-step-out-and-stride-walk
    A two-abreast-let's-glide-walk
      An arm-in-arm-let's-talk-walk
        A pigeon-and-a-bug-walk
          A-shoulder-hugging-snug-walk
            A-hot-dog-and-balloon-walk
              An-under-sun-or-moon-walk
            A-grass-grows-in-the-crack-walk
          A-rainy-day-wet-track-walk
        A place where you and I walk
      And talk and talk and talk.

—*Patricia Hubbell*

Sick

I god a liddle code doday;
id isend bery pleasand.
Da docda cape an gabe a shod,
but butha gabe a presend.

I thing I'll be in bed a dime,
ad leased dill Bunday borning.
Don't wawg in buddles in da rain—
led dis be a warding!

—*Marci Ridlon*

Grounded

I'm grounded.
I said a bad word and I'm grounded.
I just wanted to hear how it sounded.
It sounded great,
so I said it again
and taught it to my brother.
We agreed it was a *good* bad word,
but it didn't sound good to my mother!

—*Florence Parry Heide*

My Tooth Ith Loothe

My tooth ith loothe! My tooth ith loothe!
I can't go to thcool, that'th my excuthe.
I wath fine latht night when I went to bed,
But today it'th hanging by a thread!

My tooth ith loothe! My tooth ith loothe!
I'm telling you the honetht truth.
It maketh me want to jump and thout!
My tooth ith loothe....Oopth! Now it'th out!

—*George Ulrich*

Ears

Have you thought to give three cheers
For the usefulness of ears?
Ears will often spring surprises
Coming in such different sizes.
Ears are crinkled, even folded.
Ears turn pink when you are scolded.
Ears can have the oddest habits
Standing rather straight on rabbits.
Ears are little tape-recorders
Catching all the family orders.
Words, according to your mother,
Go in one and out the other.
Each side of your head you'll find them.
Don't forget to wash behind them.
Precious little thanks they'll earn you
Hearing things that don't concern you.

—*Max Fatchen*

What Someone
Said When He Was Spanked
On the Day
Before His Birthday

Some day
I may
Pack my bag and run away.
Some day
I may.
—But not today.

Some night
I might
Slip away in the moonlight.
I might.
Some night.
—But not tonight.

Some night.
Some day.
I might.
I may.
—But right now I think I'll stay.

—*John Ciardi*

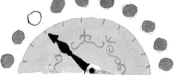

I Was Walking in a Circle

I WAS WALKING IN A CIRCLE WHEN I SPIED A PIECE OF PAPER COVERED WITH A PRETTY PICTURE COLORED YELLOW AND GREEN AND RED AS I PICKED IT UP I NOTICED THAT IT ALSO HAD SOME WRITING AND I KNEW THAT I SHOULD READ IT THIS IS WHAT THE WRITING SAID

—Jack Prelutsky

Elevator

DOWN

One wall	more.
a door,	or
the	away
others	feet
bare;	ty
no	nine-
win-	later
dow,	ment
table,	mo-
pic-	a
ture,	just
chair;	exit
a gloom-	and
y,	door
tomb-	gle
like	sin-
room,	its
and	through
small—	Enter
no	vator.
larger	ele-
than	the
a	room
show-	a
er	odd
stall.	How

UP

—Sylvia Cassedy

—Douglas Florian

Could do with legs!
Just think what we
Our pearly eggs.
Upstream we spawn
We somersault!
We vault!
We jump!
Our leaps astound!
We bound!
We spring!

The Salmon

Shakes and Ladders

As a leaning
 ladder
  climber
   there are careful
    steps to take.
     Surely nothing
      can be sadder
       if a careless
        move you make.
         Do not slither,
          do not stumble
           or your nerves
            can come unstrung
            and you well
             may take
              a tumble
               if you miss
                another rung.
                 If you're lost
                  upon a ladder
                   do not think
                    this statement
                     rude.
                      If you only
                       took
                        your bearings
                         you might learn
                          your
                           laddertude.

—*Max Fatchen*

Egg

There are
No tags, no tabs
Or wrapping paper,
Nor flaps, nor string,
Sticky tape or ribbon.
Never hidden up high
On a cupboard shelf.
Egg is a package
That can open
Itself.

—*Kristine O'Connell George*

Rolling Down a Hill

I'm rolling
rolling
rolling
down

I'm rolling
down a
hill.

I'm rolling
rolling
rolling
down

I'm rolling
down it
still.

I'm rolling
rolling
rolling
down

I'm rolling
down a
hill.

I'm rolling
rolling
down

But now
I'm feeling
ill.

—*Colin West*

43

Flags

The trees are green and thick
as if summer were here
forever,
and sun and wind and high clouds
were here forever,
except
five bright maple leaves
flag fall.

—*Ann Turner*

Afternoon on a Hill

I will be the gladdest thing
    Under the sun!
I will touch a hundred flowers
    And not pick one.

I will look at cliffs and clouds
    With quiet eyes,
Watch the wind bow down the grass,
    And the grass rise.

And when lights begin to show
    Up from the town,
I will mark which must be mine,
    And then start down!

—*Edna St. Vincent Millay*

And My Heart Soars

The beauty of the trees,
The softness of the air,
The fragrance of the grass,
    speaks to me.

The summit of the mountain,
The thunder of the sky,
The rhythm of the sea,
    speaks to me.

The faintness of the stars,
The freshness of the morning,
The dew drop on the flower,
    speaks to me.

The strength of fire,
The taste of salmon,
The trail of the sun,
And the life that never goes away,
    They speak to me.

And my heart soars.

—*Chief Dan George*

Thanksgiving

Thank You
  for all my hands can hold—
    apples red,
      and melons gold,
        yellow corn
          both ripe and sweet,
            peas and beans
              so good to eat!

Thank You
  for all my eyes can see—
    lovely sunlight,
      field and tree,
        white cloud-boats
          in sea-deep sky,
            soaring bird
              and butterfly.

Thank You
  for all my ears can hear—
    birds' song echoing
      far and near,
        songs of little
          stream, big sea,
            cricket, bullfrog,
              duck and bee!

              —*Ivy O. Eastwick*

Trees

Trees are the kindest things I know,
They do no harm, they simply grow

And spread a shade for sleepy cows,
And gather birds among their boughs.

They give us fruit in leaves above,
And wood to make our houses of,

And leaves to burn on Hallowe'en,
And in the Spring new buds of green.

They are the first when day's begun
To touch the beams of morning sun,

They are the last to hold the light
When evening changes into night,

And when a moon floats on the sky
They hum a drowsy lullaby

Of sleepy children long ago…
Trees are the kindest things I know.

              —*Harry Behn*

Reading: Summer

Summer is with it,
    she's wild,
    she likes
    bare legs and cutoffs
    and camping
    and hikes;
    she dives in deep water,
    she wades in a stream,
    she guzzles cold drinks
    and she drowns in ice cream;
    she runs barefoot,
    she picnics,
    she fishes,
    digs bait,
    she pitches a tent
    and she stays up too late
    while she counts out the stars,
    swats mosquitoes and flies,
    hears crickets,
    smells pine trees,
    spies night-creature eyes;
    she rides bareback,
    goes sailing,
    plays tennis,
    climbs trees;
    she soaks in the sunshine;
    she gulps in a breeze;
    she tastes the warm air
    on the end of her tongue,

    and she falls asleep
    reading
    alone
    in the sun.

—Myra Cohn Livingston

June

The sun is rich
    And gladly pays
In golden hours,
    Silver days,

And long green weeks
    That never end.
School's out. The time
    Is ours to spend.

There's Little League,
    Hopscotch, the creek,
And, after supper,
    Hide-and-seek.

That live-long light
    Is like a dream,
And freckles come
    Like flies to cream.

—John Updike

Turtle in July

Heavy
Heavy hot
Heavy hot hangs
Thick sticky
Icky
But I lie
Nose high
Cool pool
No fool
A turtle in July

—Marilyn Singer

August

August
  breathes
    hot
    tiger-breath
on my burning skin
and stalks me
  to the icy river
where I plunge right in.

August
  crouches
    on the bank
and steams
  in its own heat.
I'd like to drag it
  in with me
and freeze it
  ears to feet.

—Sandra Olson Liatsos

Flittermice

On leathery wings, the flittermice fly
  across the starry August sky.
I watch from my porch as they wheel by.

They rush in a stream through the hay-mow door
  of the old red barn near the sycamore,
to skim the pines and loop and soar.

Like little witches, they dodge and soar,
  then circle the sycamore tree once more.
Four swerve back, through the wide barn door.

I watch the flittermice glide and swing
  across the sky in their magic ring
and wonder how anything

wild as that
could ever be called by the plain name: "Bat."

                —*Patricia Hubbell*

All But Blind

All but blind
  In his chambered hole
Gropes for worms
  The four-clawed Mole.

All but blind
  In the evening sky
The hooded Bat
  Twirls softly by.

All but blind
  In the burning day
The Barn Owl blunders
  On her way.

And blind as are
  These three to me,
So, blind to Some-One
  I must be.

                —*Walter de la Mare*

A Bat Is Born

A bat is born
Naked and blind and pale.
His mother makes a pocket of her tail
And catches him. He clings to her long fur
By his thumbs and toes and teeth.
And then the mother dances through the night
Doubling and looping, soaring, somersaulting—
Her baby hangs on underneath.
All night, in happiness, she hunts and flies.
Her high sharp cries
Like shining needlepoints of sound
Go out into the night and, echoing back,
Tell her what they have touched.
She hears how far it is, how big it is,
Which way it's going:
She lives by hearing.
The mother eats the moths and gnats she catches
In full flight; in full flight

The mother drinks the water of the pond
She skims across. Her baby hangs on tight.
Her baby drinks the milk she makes him
In moonlight or starlight, in mid-air.
Their single shadow, printed on the moon
Or fluttering across the stars,
Whirls on all night; at daybreak
The tired mother flaps home to her rafter.
The others all are there.
They hang themselves up by their toes,
They wrap themselves in their brown wings.
Bunched upside down, they sleep in air.
Their sharp ears, their sharp teeth, their
       quick sharp faces
Are dull and slow and mild.
All the bright day, as the mother sleeps,
She folds her wings about her sleeping child.

—Randall Jarrell

Mouse Music

I can hear music,
The soft, light music,
The gentle patter of small mouse feet,
Pass through the dusk in a roundelay,
Swing through the shadows like warm gray whispers,
The thin sweet strands of gray mouse music,
Soft mouse music,
Fading away.

—Dahlov Ipcar

49

Our Panther

Our panther lies alone in the shade.
　　He doesn't even try
to taste the cool drink we have made.
　　His mouth must be so dry.

Perhaps our panther wants to be
　　back home among the trees
that bend and wave so differently
　　in such a different breeze.

—Nancy Chambers

The Hunter

A misty night
a wispy moon—
when shadows leaped
and hound dogs howled
and wild things lurked
behind one's back,
the black cat prowled
through stubbled fields.
His whiskers bristled,
body tensed, tail whipped,
and round eyes gleamed.
He was supreme.

—Ruth Tiller

The Old Dog's Song

What does the old dog say?
Well, here's another day
To sit in the sun.
And when my master's up
I'll skip around like a pup
And we'll go for a run.
But now I'll lift my head
Out of my warm bed
To greet the dawn,
Sigh gently, and slowly turn,
Slowly lie down again,
And gently yawn.

All night I've kept an eye
Open protectingly
In case of danger.
If anything had gone wrong,
I would have raised my strong
Voice in anger.
But all was safe and still.
The sun's come over the hill,
No need for warning.
When he comes down the stair
I shall be waiting there
To say Good Morning.

—Leslie Norris

Cats

Cats sleep
Anywhere,
Any table,
Any chair,
Top of piano,
Window-ledge,
In the middle,
On the edge,
Open drawer,
Empty shoe,
Anybody's
Lap will do,
Fitted in a
Cardboard box,
In the cupboard
With your frocks—
Anywhere!
They don't care!
Cats sleep
Anywhere.

—*Eleanor Farjeon*

Concerning Love

I wish she would not ask me if I love the
    Kitten more than her.
Of Course I love her. But I love the Kitten,
    too; and It has Fur.

—*Josephine Preston Peabody*

51

Eletelephony

Once there was an elephant,
Who tried to use the telephant—
No! no! I mean an elephone
Who tried to use the telephone—
(Dear me! I am not certain quite
That even now I've got it right.)

Howe'er it was, he got his trunk
Entangled in the telephunk;
The more he tried to get it free,
The louder buzzed the telephee—
(I fear I'd better drop the song
Of elephop and telephong!)

—*Laura E. Richards*

Hippopotamus

Hooray for the hippopotamus—
A most enormous beast;
He looks as though he's eaten
Just a little too much yeast.
His mouth would dwarf a canyon
(And that's the honest truth!)—
Why, it takes three dozen dentists
Just to pull a hippo's tooth.

—*Gail Kredenser*

Brachiosaurus

This dinosaur is now extinct
While I am still extant.
I'd like to bring it back alive.
                    (Unhappily I can't.)
The largest ones weighed fifty tons
And stood three stories high.
Their dinner ration? Vegetation.
                    (Never hurt a fly.)
Alas! Alack! They're dead and gone
Through failure to adapt
And only known by track and bone.
                    (I wish we'd overlapped.)

—*Mary Ann Hoberman*

Dinosaurs

Dinosaurs
Do not count,
Because
They are all
Dead:

None of us
Saw them, dogs
Do not even
Know that
They were there—

But they
Still walk
About heavily
In everybody's
Head.

—*Valerie Worth*

Building a Skyscraper

They're building a skyscraper
Near our street.
Its height will be nearly
One thousand feet.

It covers completely
A city block.
They drilled its foundation
Through solid rock.

They made its framework
Of great steel beams
With riveted joints
And welded seams.

A swarm of workmen
Strain and strive
Like busy bees
In a honeyed hive

Building the skyscraper
Into the air
While crowds of people
Stand and stare.

Higher and higher
The tall towers rise
Like Jacob's ladder
Into the skies.

—*James S. Tippett*

Skyscraper

Skyscraper, skyscraper,
Scrape me some sky:
Tickle the sun
While the stars go by.

Tickle the stars
While the sun's climbing high,
Then skyscraper, skyscraper,
Scrape me some sky.

—*Dennis Lee*

Ditchdiggers

Like lean giraffes about the building site,
With questing noses tilted to the sky,
They stand, a still and silent little herd,
And let the world go by…

Until the whistle blows. And then they turn
With lowered heads, travel and work and wheel,
Grabbing great gobbets of the yellow clay
To toss it into trucks, tireless as steel…

Until the whistle blows again. And then,
With noses tilted up against the sky,
They stand, a still and silent little herd,
And let the world go by.

—*Lydia Pender*

The Seal

How must it feel
to be
a
seal
and swish among the
ducks
and teal
and swim
a cool
Virginia Reel
right underneath
somebody's
keel?
Then
much
to
somebody's surprise
pop up your head
right out of sea
and blink your big blue baby eyes
and flap your fins
with glee?
And o what bliss
on summer days
what bliss it is
to lie and laze
on a warm mudflat
in the sun
and *sunbathe*
just
like
anyone.
I think the seal
has
all
the
fun.

—Conrad Aiken

Crab Dance

Play moonlight
and the red crabs dance
their scuttle-foot dance
on the mud-packed beach

Play moonlight
and the red crabs dance
their sideways dance
to the soft-sea beat

Play moonlight
and the red crabs dance
their bulb-eye dance
their last crab dance

—Grace Nichols

When Whales Exhale
(Whale Watching)

There's a horn sound
from the blowhole
and a high-speed spout
when a whale at sea
blasts the old air out.
It breathes up a geyser,
a flare of fizz,
a white cloud that shows you
where it is
in the endless waves
of the great green sea.
Oh, whales exhale
magnificently!

—Constance Levy

Octopus

The octopus is one tough cuss
With muscles built like truckers'—
It lifts great weights in several arms,
Each lined with sticky suckers.

If you should meet an octopus
That greets you, "Hi—let's shake!"
You'll stand a long while wondering
Which tentacle to take.

—X. J. Kennedy

The Sandpiper

At the edge of tide
He stops to wonder,
Races through
The lace of thunder.

On toothpick legs
Swift and brittle,
He runs and pipes
And his voice is little.

But small or not,
He has a notion
To outshout
The Atlantic Ocean.

—Frances Frost

Wilderness Rivers

There are rivers
that I know,
born of ice
and melting snow,
white with rapids,
swift to roar,
with no farms
along their shore,
with no cattle
come to drink
at a staid
and welcoming brink,
with no millwheel,
ever turning,
in that cold
relentless churning.

Only deer
and bear and mink
at those shallows
come to drink,
only paddles,
swift and light,
flick that current
in their flight.
I have felt
my heart beat high,
watching
with exultant eye,
those pure rivers
which have known
no will, no purpose
but their own.

—*Elizabeth Coatsworth*

River in Winter

The ice moves slowly
                    down the river
the gulls
        are circling
                    high
grey and white
grey and white
against
        the
            grey-blue
                    sky!

—*Charlotte Zolotow*

Undecided

The sun sprays
summery light
but the wind speaks
with winter's tongue.

The pond reflects
so much cloudy blue
I can't quite decide
whether it's the sky

using the pond
as a mirror
or the pond wearing
bracelets of sky.

—*Ralph Fletcher*

Sky, Sea, Shore

Stars in a frosty sky
Crackle and blaze;
Streams in the lowland meadows
Linger and laze;
Shells on the seashore gleam,
Washed by the tide;
Seagulls over the harbor
Circle and glide.
    Blue smoke and prancing steed,
    Swallow and snake and swan—
    How many more
    Curving, glistening S-things
    In sky, sea, shore?

—James Reeves

Breakers

Roaring,
all flowing grace,
the water tigers pounce,
feed on the shore,
worry it
again and again,
take great bites
they cannot swallow
and leave the toothmarks
of their long white fangs.

—Lillian Morrison

Until I Saw the Sea

Until I saw the sea
I did not know
that wind
could wrinkle water so.

I never knew
that sun
could splinter a whole sea of blue.

Nor
did I know before,
a sea breathes in and out
upon a shore.

—Lilian Moore

Forethought

The sea is very large indeed
And pretty nicely planned;
For where there is no sea, you see,
It leaves a place for land.

—George Reiter Brill

59

The Farmer

A plot of weeds,
an old grey mule.
Hot sun and sweat
on a bright Southern day.
Strong, stern papa
under a straw hat,
plowing and planting
his whole life away.
His backbone is forged
of African Iron
and red Georgia clay.

—*Carole Boston Weatherford*

You Never Hear the Garden Grow

Row on row,
you never hear the garden
grow.

Seeds split.
Roots shove and reach.
Earth heaves.

Leaves unfurl.
Stems pierce the
ground.

Pea pods fatten.
Vines
stretch and curl.

Such growing
going on
without a sound!

—*Lilian Moore*

Scarecrow Complains

It's garden gossip
all day
long

cricket chatter
bee buzz babble

loud
bird song.

I look fierce
but ah, they
know.

I stand
tall
but they all
know.

I'm only
straw.
Can't scare a
crow.

—*Lilian Moore*

60

A Homely Winter Idyl

Great, long, lean clouds in sullen host
Along the skyline passed today;
While overhead I've only seen
A leaden sky the whole day long.

My heart would gloomily have mused
Had I not seen those queer, old crows
Stop short in their mad frolicking
And pose for me in long, black rows.

—*Carl Sandburg*

The Happy Hedgehog

The happiness of hedgehogs
Lies in complete repose.
They spend the months of winter
In a long delicious doze;
And if they note the time at all
They think 'How fast it goes!'

—*E. V. Rieu*

Merry Christmas

I saw on the snow
when I tried my skis
the track of a mouse
beside some trees.

Before he tunneled
to reach his house
he wrote "Merry Christmas"
in white, in mouse.

—*Aileen Fisher*

61

The Toaster

A silver-scaled Dragon with jaws flaming red
Sits at my elbow and toasts my bread.
I hand him fat slices, and then, one by one,
He hands them back when he sees they are done.

—*William Jay Smith*

Channel Changer

We have a billion stations.
We have cable and of course
a satellite night hookup
with a backup power source.

We have a giant screen TV
with Dolby surround sound.
That darn remote control thing,
though, never can be found.

That's why a Channel Changer
is a pet beyond compare.
He surfs through the commercials
and he never needs repair.

His ears are each antennas.
His one eye is open wide.
I never have to walk him
since he hates to go outside.

He doesn't get much exercise
but anyone can tell he
loves to press each button
on his eighty-button belly.

—*Richard Michelson*

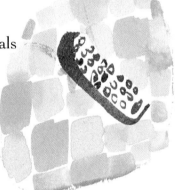

How to Assemble a Toy

This is the whatsit that fits on the knob
Of the gadget that turns the thingamabob.
This is the dingus that fits in place
With the doodad next to the whosiface.
This is the jigger that goes in the hole
Where the gizmo turns the rigamarole.
Now slip the ding-dang into the slot
Of the jugamalug, and what have you got?

It's a genuine neverwas such a not!

—*John Ciardi*

Taking Off

The airplane taxis down the field
And heads into the breeze,
It lifts its wheels above the ground,
It skims above the trees,
It rises high and higher
Away up toward the sun,
It's just a speck against the sky
—And now it's gone!

—*Mary McB. Green*

A Modern Dragon

A train is a dragon that roars through the dark.
He wriggles his tail as he sends up a spark.
He pierces the night with his one yellow eye,
And all the earth trembles when he rushes by.

—*Rowena Bastin Bennett*

Buses

Fat and cross, the city buses,
sometimes late and sometimes early,
grunt like hippopotamuses
in the traffic's hurly-burly.

Huffy hippos, nose to tail,
lined up on the river banks,
blink along the narrow trail,
nudging one another's flanks.

—*Maxine Kumin*

Limo

Come now, every her and him-o, be you fat or be you slim-o;
glad or grim-o; smart or dim-o; loud or prim-o; wide or trim-o;
full of vig or full of vim-o. Cherubim and Seraphim-o, gather
every life and limb-o; sing a psalm-o, sing a hymn-o, as you pile
up to the brim-o, as you pile up to the rim-o, as you pile into my
limo — lengthy, lissome, limber limo — pile into my new stretch limo.

—*Sylvia Cassedy*

The Bad-Mood Bug

I don't know what I want today
But nothing feels quite right.
If I had an ice-cream pie
I wouldn't take a bite.

I wouldn't ride a water slide
Climb monkey bars or trees,
No games, no toys, no magic wands,
No elephants for me.

There's a grouchy bug inside me
And it's usually asleep,
But when the grumpy thing wakes up
I turn into a creep.

—*Brod Bagert*

Mad Song

I shut my door
To keep you out
Won't do no good
To stand and shout
Won't listen to
A thing you say
Just time you took
Yourself away
I lock my door
To keep me here
Until I'm sure
You disappear.

—*Myra Cohn Livingston*

Some People

Isn't it strange some people make
You feel so tired inside,
Your thoughts begin to shrivel up
Like leaves all brown and dried!

But when you're with some other ones,
It's stranger still to find
Your thoughts as thick as fireflies
All shiny in your mind!

—*Rachel Field*

When I Was Lost

Underneath my belt
My stomach was a stone.
Sinking was the way I felt.
And hollow.
And Alone.

—*Dorothy Aldis*

Moving

We are moving away
So I must say good-bye
To my room and my swing
And that sweet part of sky
That sometimes hangs blue
And sometimes hangs gray
Over the fields
Where I used to play.
Good-bye to my old friends
Jason and Sue
They wave from their porches,
Are they crying too?
The moving truck rumbles
Past all that I know—
The school and the woods
And the creek down below.
And everything seems
To be pleading
"Don't go!"

—*Eileen Spinelli*

Autumn Night Music

Summer is waning;
nights are gaining.
Evening trees have lost their song.
Katydids, the last to strum,
are packing up and moving on.

Music lovers, don't despair!
Autumn tunes are in the air.
Just tonight I heard a breeze
practicing inside the trees.

There is music after summer
with a different kind of strummer!

—*Constance Levy*

September

The breezes taste
  Of apple peel.
The air is full
  Of smells to feel—

Ripe fruit, old footballs,
  Drying grass,
New books and blackboard
  Chalk in class.

The bee, his hive
  Well-honeyed, hums
While Mother cuts
  Chrysanthemums.

Like plates washed clean
  With suds, the days
Are polished with
  A morning haze.

—*John Updike*

Autumn

Now the summer is grown old
the light long summer
            is grown old.

Leaves change
and the garden is gold
with marigolds and zinnias
tangled and bold
blazing blazing
orange and gold.

     The light long summer
     is grown old.

—*Charlotte Zolotow*

Something Told the Wild Geese

Something told the wild geese
    It was time to go.
Though the fields lay golden
    Something whispered — "Snow."
Leaves were green and stirring,
    Berries, luster-glossed,
But beneath warm feathers
    Something cautioned — "Frost."
All the sagging orchards
    Steamed with amber spice,
But each wild breast stiffened
    At remembered ice.
Something told the wild geese
    It was time to fly —
Summer sun was on their wings,
    Winter in their cry.

—Rachel Field

Pumpkin Picking

Let's go picking in the pumpkin patch.
Now we're jiggling the old gate latch.
Gate swings wide and we step inside.
Pumpkins spread like an ocean tide.
You take the one like a fat balloon.
I'll take the one like an orange moon.
Hike to the house in fifty paces.
Then we'll carve out the pumpkin faces.

—Sandra Olson Liatsos

Autumn Woods

I like the woods
    In autumn
When dry leaves hide the ground,
When the trees are bare
And the wind sweeps by
With a lonesome rushing sound.

I can rustle the leaves
    In autumn
And I can make a bed
In the thick dry leaves
That have fallen
From the bare trees
Overhead.

—James S. Tippett

September

I already know where Africa is
and I already know how to
count to ten and
I went to school every day last year,
why do I have to go again?

—*Lucille Clifton*

Monday!

Overslept
Rain is pouring
Missed the bus
Dad is roaring
Late for school
Forgot my spelling
Soaking wet
Clothes are smelling
Dropped my books
Got them muddy
Flunked a test
Didn't study
Teacher says
I must do better
Lost my money
Tore my sweater
Feeling dumber
Feeling glummer
Monday sure can be
A bummer.

—*David L. Harrison*

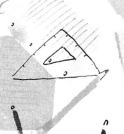

New Notebook

Lines
in a new notebook
run, even and fine,
like telephone wires
across a snowy landscape.

With wet, black strokes
the alphabet settles between them,
comfortable as a flock of crows.

—*Judith Thurman*

Today

Today I will not live up to my potential.
Today I will not relate well to my peer group.
Today I will not contribute in class.
    I will not volunteer one thing.
Today I will not strive to do better.
Today I will not achieve or adjust or grow enriched
    or get involved.
I will not put up my hand even if the teacher is wrong
    and I can prove it.

Today I might eat the eraser off my pencil.
I'll look at clouds.
I'll be late.
I don't think I'll wash.

I need a rest.

—*Jean Little*

Homework

Homework sits on top of Sunday, squashing Sunday flat.
Homework has the smell of Monday, homework's very fat
Heavy books and piles of paper, answers I don't know.
Sunday evening's almost finished, now I'm going to go
Do my homework in the kitchen. Maybe just a snack,
Then I'll sit right down and start as soon as I run back
For some chocolate sandwich cookies. Then I'll really do
All that homework in a minute. First I'll see what new
Show they've got on television in the living room.
Everybody's laughing there, but misery and gloom
And a full refrigerator are where I am at.
I'll just have another sandwich. Homework's very fat.

—*Russell Hoban*

69

Poem to Mud

Poem to mud—
Poem to ooze—
Patted in pies, or coating your shoes.

Poem to slooze—
Poem to crud—
Fed by a leak, or spread by a flood.
Wherever, whenever, whyever it goes,
Stirred by your finger, or strained by your toes,
There's nothing sloppier, slipperier, floppier,
There's nothing slickier, stickier, thickier,
There's nothing quickier to make grown-ups sickier,
Trulier coolier,
Than wonderful mud.

—Zilpha Keatly Snyder

What Is Black?

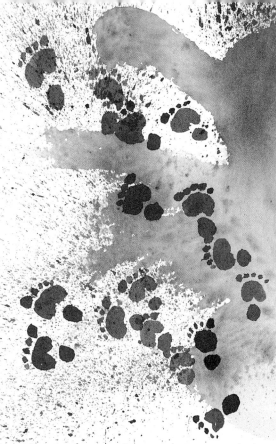

Black is the night
When there isn't a star
And you can't tell by looking
Where you are.
Black is a pail of paving tar.
Black is jet
And things you'd like to forget.
Black is a smokestack
Black is a cat,
A leopard, a raven,
A high silk hat.
The sound of black is
"Boom! Boom! Boom!"
Echoing in
An empty room.

Black is kind—
It covers up
The run-down street,
The broken cup.

Black is charcoal
And patio grill,
The soot spots on
The window sill.
Black is a feeling
Hard to explain
Like suffering but
Without the pain.
Black is licorice
And patent leather shoes
Black is the print
In the news.
Black is beauty
In its deepest form,
The darkest cloud
In a thunderstorm.
Think of what starlight
And lamplight would lack
Diamonds and fireflies
If they couldn't lean against
Black....

—Mary O'Neill

hist whist

hist   whist
little ghostthings
tip-toe
twinkle-toe

little twitchy
witches and tingling
goblins
hob-a-nob   hob-a-nob

little hoppy happy
toad in tweeds
tweeds
little itchy mousies

with scuttling
eyes   rustle and run   and
hidehidehide
whisk

whisk   look out for the old woman
with the wart on her nose
what she'll do to yer
nobody knows

for she knows the devil   ooch
the devil   ouch
the devil
ach   the great

green
dancing
devil
devil

devil
devil

wheeEEE

—*e. e. cummings*

71

Desert Snow

Coyote spies
new moon, slight
grin, high
in the sky.

Coyote licks
cold, white
shine, mouthful
of stars.

Coyote serenades
moon, grinning slyly
at hills sleeping in starry blankets,
at music rising, "Halloooooooooo!"

—*Pat Mora*

Spell of the Moon

Owl floats through the midnight wood
His terrible voice.
Small creatures alive on the ground
Keep still as ice,
Afraid their bones will be snapped
In his talon's vice.

But the moon hangs in the air,
In the tree's arms,
And she throws on trees and ground
Her silver charms,
Healing the fear of the dark
And night's alarms.

The fox to his lair in the dark
Through shadows will slip,
The shrew and the mole and the vole
To safety creep,
And the moon rides silent and high.
And the wood's asleep.

—*Leslie Norris*

I Don't Believe in Bigfoot

I don't believe in Bigfoot
Or skeletons that dance.
I don't believe in werewolves
Or zombies in a trance.
I don't believe in Martians
Or ghosts in sheets of white.
I don't believe in witches,
Who ride their brooms at night.
I don't believe in vampires
Or monsters from the sea —
And I'm hoping with my fingers crossed
They don't believe in me.

—Eileen Spinelli

Eyes

In the darkness of the hall
Tiny eyes are watching me,
Shining sparks of silvered green
Watching, watching me.

Look! the cupboard has closed.
Wee, small hands, quick finger tipped,
Slipped the key out of the lock.

Nimble legs go scurrying by,
Bramble flecked in cobweb green
Whisk away before half seen.

—J. Paget-Fredericks

Moths and Moonshine

Moths and moonshine mean to me
Magic — madness — mystery.

Witches dancing weird and wild
Mischief make for man and child.

Owls screech from woodland shades,
Moths glide through moonlit glades,

Moving in dark and secret wise
Like a plotter in disguise.

Moths and moonshine mean to me
Magic — madness — mystery.

— James Reeves

73

Noodles

Noodles for breakfast,
Noodles for lunch,
Noodles for dinner,
Noodles that crunch,
Noodles to twirl,
Noodles to slurp—
I could eat noodles
all day!   Burp!

—Janet S. Wong

Spinach

One thing I really, really hate
is seeing spinach on my plate!
   It's oozy, it's wiggly,
   it's icky, it's squiggly,
   it's greasy, it's grimy,
   it's sticky, it's slimy,
and as it slithers ever closer
it gets slimier and grosser.

This is the thing that worries me:
I don't like spinach,
but spinach likes ME!
And as it sits upon the plate
it's thinking *I* am looking great.
Here I sit and now I see
if I don't eat it,
it will eat ME!

—Florence Parry Heide

Chocolate
Chocolate

Chocolate
Chocolate
              i
love
          you so
          i
want
       to
marry
       you
       and
live
       forever
          in the
          flavor
of your
   brown

—Arnold Adoff

The Potato Versus the Pea

One potato
makes a meal.
One pea…
no big deal.

—Dee Lillegard

Alligator Pie

Alligator pie, alligator pie,
If I don't get some I think I'm gonna die.
Give away the green grass, give away the sky,
But don't give away my alligator pie.

Alligator stew, alligator stew,
If I don't get some I don't know what I'll do.
Give away my furry hat, give away my shoe,
But don't give away my alligator stew.

Alligator soup, alligator soup,
If I don't get some I think I'm gonna droop.
Give away my hockey stick, give away my hoop,
But don't give away my alligator soup.

—*Dennis Lee*

What You Don't Know About Food

Jelly's made from jellyfish.
Spaghetti's really worms.
Ice cream's just some dirty snow
mixed up with grimy germs.
Bread is made of glue and paste.
So are cakes and pies.
Peanut butter's filled with stuff
like squashed-up lizard eyes.
And as you eat potato chips,
remember all the while—
they're slices of the dried-up brain
of some old crocodile.

—*Florence Parry Heide*

75

Norman Norton's Nostrils

Oh, Norman Norton's nostrils
Are powerful and strong;
Hold on to your belongings
If he should come along.

And do not ever let him
Inhale with all his might,
Or else your pens and pencils
Will disappear from sight.

Right up his nose they'll vanish;
Your future will be black.
Unless he gets the sneezes
You'll *never* get them back!

—*Colin West*

Slicing Salami

The strangest strange stranger I've met in my life
Was the man who made use of his nose as a knife.
He'd slice up salami, tomatoes and cheese
At the tip of his nose with phenomenal ease.
He'd buy food in bulk at incredible prices
And then use his nose to reduce it to slices.
His wife ran away and I know that he'll miss her.
The woman was frightened that one day he'd kiss her.

—*Denise Rodgers*

Sneeze

There's a
sort of a
tickle
the size of a
nickel,
a bit like the
prickle
of sweet-sour
pickle;

it's a
quivery
shiver
the shape of a
sliver,
like eels in a
river;

a kind of a
wiggle
that starts as a
jiggle
and joggles
its way to a
tease,

which I
cannot
suppress
any longer,
I guess,
so pardon me,
please,
while I
sneeze.

—*Maxine Kumin*

Be Glad Your Nose Is on Your Face

Be glad your nose is on your face,
not pasted on some other place,
for if it were where it is not,
you might dislike your nose a lot.

Imagine if your precious nose
were sandwiched in between your toes,
that clearly would not be a treat,
for you'd be forced to smell your feet.

Your nose would be a source of dread
were it attached atop your head,
it soon would drive you to despair,
forever tickled by your hair.

Within your ear, your nose would be
an absolute catastrophe,
for when you were obliged to sneeze,
your brain would rattle from the breeze.

Your nose, instead, through thick and thin,
remains between your eyes and chin,
not pasted on some other place—
be glad your nose is on your face!

—Jack Prelutsky

77

Tree Climbing

This is my tree,
my place to be alone in,
my branches for climbing,
my green leaves for hiding in,
my sunshine for reading,
my clouds for dreaming,
my sky for singing,
my tree, my beautiful tree.

—*Kathleen Fraser*

The Secret Place

There's a place I go, inside myself,
    Where nobody else can be,
And none of my friends can tell it's there—
    Nobody knows but me.

It's hard to explain the way it feels,
    Or even where I go.
It isn't a place in time or space,
    But once I'm there, I *know.*

It's tiny, it's shiny, it can't be seen,
    But it's big as the sky at night…
I try to explain and it hurts my brain,
    But once I'm there, it's *right.*

There's a place I know inside myself,
    And it's neither big nor small,
And whenever I go, it feels as though
    I never left at all.

—*Dennis Lee*

Secrets

I had a little secret,
My very, very first;
I tried so hard to keep it,
I thought my heart would burst.

And then I told my secret,
And all the charm was lost;
Next time I'll keep my secret,
No matter what the cost.

—*Emilie Fendall Johnson*

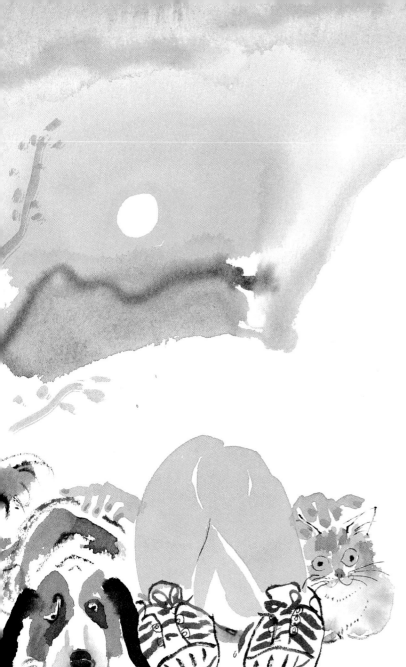

This Is My Rock

This is my rock,
And here I run
To steal the secret of the sun;

This is my rock,
And here come I
Before the night has swept the sky;

This is my rock,
This is the place
I meet the evening face to face.

—David McCord

Robert, Who Is Often
A Stranger to Himself

Do you ever look in the looking-glass
And see a stranger there?
A child you know and do not know,
Wearing what you wear?

—Gwendolyn Brooks

Just Three

How very quiet things can be,
With just the dog, the cat, and me.
There's no one else to laugh and shout,
To dance and sing and run about.
With just the dog, the cat, and me,
How very quiet things can be.

—William Wise

79

Tiger

The tiger
Has swallowed
A black sun,

In his cold
Cage he
Carries it still:

Black flames
Flicker through
His fur,

Black rays roar
From the centers
Of his eyes.

— *Valerie Worth*

The Lion Cub

My fur is soft. I am not a lion yet.
You can tease me a little, treat me like a pet.

The keeper is feeding my parents. Trust me to
Be playful. I can warm and comfort you.

Forget the forests and jungle, the great sun-face
Of my father. He has violence and grace

And I have neither yet. For a little time
I am a prince locked safe in a nursery rhyme.

—*Elizabeth Jennings*

The Lion

The lion just adores to eat
A lot of red and tender meat,
And if you ask the lion what
Is much the tenderest of the lot,
He will not say a roast of lamb
Or curried beef or devilled ham
Or crispy pork or corned beef hash
Or sausages or mutton mash.
Then could it be a big plump hen?
He answers no. What is it, then?
Oh, lion dear, could I not make
You happy with a lovely steak?
Could I entice you from your lair
With rabbit-pie or roasted hare?
The lion smiled and shook his head.
He came up very close and said,
"The meat I am about to chew
Is neither steak nor chops. IT'S YOU."

—*Roald Dahl*

81

We Are Plooters

We are Plooters,
We don't care,
We make messes
Everywhere,
We strip forests
Bare of trees,
We dump garbage
In the seas.

We are Plooters,
We enjoy
Finding beauty
To destroy,
We intrude
Where creatures thrive,
Soon there's little
Left alive.

Underwater,
Underground,
Nothing's safe
When we're around,
We spew poisons
In the air,
We are Plooters,
We don't care.

—*Jack Prelutsky*

Breaks Free

I just want to be
where the earth breaks free
of concrete and metal and glass,
of asphalt and plastic and gas,
where sun is king
and water is queen,
where cactus grow tall
and the air is clean.
I just want to be
where the earth breaks free
of fences and alleys and walls,
of factories and traffic and malls,
where owls sleep
in the heart of day
waiting for sunset
to hunt their prey,
where mountains rise
in seas of sand
and coyotes roam
across the land.

—*Frank Asch*

Sea Song

Shell,
so cleverly curled,
sing me a sea song!

Tell me tales
of dolphins
cavorting   of
great whales snorting,
bright fish
flashing
their scales.

What song do you
bring
to me, Shell?

Only this—
for all who live
in the waters
of the
world,
I sing of their longing,
"Unpoison the sea!"

—*Lilian Moore*

Will We Ever See?

Will we ever see a tiger again,
stalking its prey with shining eyes?

Will we see the giant orangutan
inspecting its mate for fleas?

Or a California condor
feeding on the side of a hill?

Or a whooping crane
walking softly through a salty marsh?

Or hear the last of the blue whales
singing its sad song under the deep water?

—*Georgia Heard*

Prayer for Earth

Last night
an owl
called from the hill.
Coyotes howled.
A deer stood still
nibbling at bushes far away.
The moon shone silver.
Let this stay.

Today
two noisy crows
flew by,
their shadows pasted to the sky.
The sun broke out
through clouds of gray.
An iris opened.
Let this stay.

—*Myra Cohn Livingston*

Uggle

Uggle is a blanket
Worn to shreds
It's been on every
One of my beds.
Once it went off
In a Good Will pack
And I had an awful time
Getting it back.
Once it was tossed
In an old trash bin
But I saw its fringe
And climbed right in.
Once it was bitten
By a moth
And once it was used
As a dusting cloth!
Why did I love it
More than my cat,
My dog, my doll and my
Sunday hat?
Because when dark
Night shadows flung
Monsters on walls
When I was young
It was to Uggle
That I clung....
Later when I
Was four or five
And *knew* that
Shadows weren't alive
Uggle was part
Of every night
Like the stars and
The bedside light,
Like loving eyes and
A hand held tight....
Like somebody, almost,
But not quite....

—*Mary O'Neill*

A Good Place to Sleep

Little bear sleeps in the woods, in the woods.
Little gull sleeps on the sea.
Little colt sleeps in a big, big field.
Little squirrel sleeps in a tree.
Small fox sleeps in a den, in a den.
A hive is the place for a bee.
But here am I in my very own bed,
And that's the best place for me.

—*Margaret Hillert*

Flashlight

Tucked tight in bed, the day all gone,
I like to click my flashlight on,
Then climb in under with my feet
And shine a moon out through the sheet.

I'll throw a circle on the wall,
Move close up to it, make it small,
And then yank back and make that moon
Blow up—an instant light-balloon!

Each flashlight battery, slid out,
Looks piglike with a silver snout
And like two pigs parading, they
Need to line up and look one way.

Ben Franklin with a kite and key
Attracted electricity,
But they must not be also-rans
Who put up light in little cans.

—*X. J. Kennedy*

If a Bad Dream Comes

If a bad dream comes
and scares me awake,
I pull the covers over my head
and hide
inside
the small warm room
of my bed.

My blanket is a ceiling.
My mattress is a floor.
The covers tucked tight
are the corners of the walls.
And my pillow is a door
that I can lock
against
the night.

It's dark in this room,
and it almost feels safe,
but if someone should come
to see if I'm awake,
if someone should ask
"Who is hiding there?"
I'd say:
"It's me—and I'm scared."

—*Siv Cedering Fox*

Covers

Glass covers windows
    to keep the cold away
Clouds cover the sky
    to make a rainy day

Nighttime covers
    all the things that creep
Blankets cover me
    when I'm asleep

—*Nikki Giovanni*

At the Library

I flip the pages of a book and slip inside,
where crystal seas await and pirates hide.
I find a paradise where birds can talk,
where children fly and trees prefer to walk.
Sometimes I end up on a city street.
I recognize the brownskin girl I meet.
She's skinny, but she's strong, and brave, and wise.
I smile because I see *me* in her eyes.

—*Nikki Grimes*

A Poem Is a Little Path

A poem is a little path
That leads you through the trees.
It takes you to the cliffs and shores,
To anywhere you please.

Follow it and trust your way
With mind and heart as one,
And when the journey's over,
You'll find you've just begun.

—*Charles Ghigna*

Eating While Reading

What is better
Than this book
And the churn of candy
In your mouth,
Or the balloon of bubble gum,
Or the crack of sunflower seeds,
Or the swig of soda,
Or the twist of beef jerky,
Or the slow slither
Of snow cone syrup
Running down your arms?

What is better than
This sweet dance
On the tongue,
And this book
That pulls you in?
It yells, *"Over here!"*
And you hurry along
With a red, sticky face.

—*Gary Soto*

Keep a Poem in Your Pocket

Keep a poem in your pocket
and a picture in your head
and you'll never feel lonely
at night when you're in bed.

The little poem will sing to you
the little picture bring to you
a dozen dreams to dance to you
at night when you're in bed.

So—
Keep a poem in your pocket
and a picture in your head
and you'll never feel lonely
at night when you're in bed.

—*Beatrice Schenk de Regniers*

When You Can Read

When you can read, then you can go
from Kalamazoo to Idaho—
Or read directions that explain
just how to build a model plane—
Or bake a cake or cook a stew—
The words will tell you what to do!
When you can read, then you can play
a brand new game the proper way—
Or get a letter from a friend
and read it…to the very end.

—*Bobbi Katz*

Index of Titles

The date in brackets following the title is the year of original publication

Index of Authors

Acknowledgments

Grateful acknowledgment is made to the following for permission to reprint previously published material:

Addison Wesley Longman for "Ears Hear" by Lucia M. and James L. Hymes Jr., from *Oodles for Noodles*. © 1964 Lucia and James Hymes Jr. Reprinted by permission of Addison Wesley Longman.

Authors' Licensing & Collecting Society, Ltd. (A.L.C.S. Ltd.) for "The Happy Hedgehog" by E. V. Rieu from *The Flattered Flying Fish*. © 1962 by E. V. Rieu. Reprinted by kind permission of A.L.C.S. Ltd. on behalf of the estate of E. V. Rieu.

Bantam Doubleday Dell Publishing Group, Inc., for "If Only" from *The Word Party* by Richard Edwards and John Lawrence, illustrator. Copyright © 1986 by Richard Edwards. Used by permission of Delacorte Press, a division of Bantam Doubleday Dell Publishing Group, Inc. "Oh, to Be…" from *A Mouse in My Roof* by Richard Edwards. Copyright © 1988 by Richard Edwards. Used by permission of Delacorte Press, a division of Bantam Doubleday Dell Publishing Group, Inc. "Breakfast" from *The Other Side of the Door* by Jeff Moss. Copyright © 1991 by Jeff Moss. Used by permission of Bantam Books, a division of Bantam Doubleday Dell Publishing Group, Inc. "What Is Black?" copyright © 1960 by Curtis Publishing Company from *Hailstones and Halibut Bones* by Mary O'Neill and Leonard Weisgard, illustrator. Used by permission of Doubleday, a division of Bantam Doubleday Dell Publishing Group, Inc. "The Lizard" copyright © 1961 by Beatrice Roethke, Administratrix of the Estate of Theodore Roethke. From *The Collected Poems of Theodore Roethke* by Theodore Roethke. Used by permission of Doubleday, a division of Bantam Doubleday Dell Publishing Group, Inc. "Beetles" from *Goose Grass Rhymes* by Monica Shannon. Copyright © 1930 by Doubleday, a division of Bantam Doubleday Dell Publishing Group, Inc. "My Tooth Ith Loothe" from *My Tooth Ith Loothe* by George Ulrich. Copyright © 1995 by George Ulrich. Used by permission of Bantam Doubleday Dell Books for Young Readers.

The Estate of Rowena B. Bennett for "A Modern Dragon" from *Songs from Around a Toadstool Table* copyright © 1967 by Rowena Bastin Bennett. Reprinted by permission of Kenneth C. Bennett.

Boyds Mills Press for "The Bad-Mood Bug" from *Chicken Socks* by Brod Bagert. Copyright © 1993 Brod Bagert. Published by Boyds Mills Press. "Rain Sizes" from *The Reason* by John Ciardi. Copyright © 1994 by John Ciardi. Published by Boyds Mills Press. "What Someone Said When He Was Spanked on the Day Before His Birthday" from *You Know Who* by John Ciardi. Copyright © 1964 by John Ciardi. Copyright renewed 1991 by Judith

H. Ciardi. Published by Boyds Mills Press. "A Circle of Sun," "Dragonfly," and "Jacks" from *Lemonade Sun* by Rebecca Kai Dotlich. Copyright © 1998 by Rebecca Kai Dotlich. Published by Boyds Mills Press. "Monday!" from *Somebody Catch My Homework* by David L. Harrison. Copyright © 1993 by David L. Harrison. Published by Boyds Mills Press. "Will We Ever See?" from *Earth, Sea, and Sky* by Georgia Heard. Copyright © 1992 by Georgia Heard. Published by Boyds Mills Press. "A Good Place to Sleep" from *The Sky Is Not So Far Away* by Margaret Hillert. Copyright © 1996 by Margaret Hillert. Published by Boyds Mills Press. "August" and "Pumpkin Picking" from *Bicycle Riding* by Sandra Olson Liatsos. Copyright © 1997 by Sandra Olson Liatsos. Published by Boyds Mills Press. "Breakers" and "Rain Sound" from *Whistling the Morning In* by Lillian Morrison. Copyright © 1992 by Lillian Morrison. Published by Boyds Mills Press. "Running Song" and "Sick" from *Sun Through the Window* by Marci Ridlon. Copyright © 1969, 1996 by Marci Ridlon McGill. Published by Boyds Mills Press. "I Don't Believe in Bigfoot" and "Moving" from *Where Is the Night Train Going?* by Eileen Spinelli. Copyright © 1996 by Eileen Spinelli. Published by Boyds Mills Press. Reprinted by permission of Boyds Mills Press.

Brandt & Brandt Literary Agents, Inc., for "The Seal" from *Cats and Bats and Things with Wings* by Conrad Aiken. Copyright © 1965 by Conrad Aiken. Copyright renewed © 1993 Joan Aiken and Jane Aiken Hodge. "The Old Dog's Song" from *Merlin and the Snake Egg* by Leslie Norris, the Viking Press. Copyright © 1978 by Leslie Norris. "Spell of the Moon" from *Merlin and the Snake Egg* by Leslie Norris, the Viking Press. Copyright © 1978 by Leslie Norris. Reprinted by permission of Brandt & Brandt Literary Agents, Inc.

Curtis Brown Group, Ltd., for "At the Bottom of the Garden" from *Asana and the Animals* by Grace Nichols. Copyright Grace Nichols 1994, 1998. "Crab Dance" from *Come on into My Tropical Garden* by Grace Nichols. Copyright Grace Nichols 1994, 1998. Reprinted by permission of Curtis Brown Group, Ltd., London, on behalf of Grace Nichols. "My Name Is…" from *Silver Bells and Cockle Shells* by Pauline Clarke. © Pauline Clarke 1962. "Just Three" by William Wise. From *All on a Summer's Day* (Pantheon Books). Copyright © 1971 by William Wise. "Spells" by Jane Yolen from *Best Witches, Poems for Halloween* (G. P. Putnam's Sons). Copyright © 1989 by Jane Yolen. Reprinted by permission of Curtis Brown Group, Ltd.

Edward S. Cassedy Jr. for "Elevator," by Sylvia Cassedy from *Roomrimes* (Thomas Y. Crowell Co., © 1987 by Sylvia Cassedy). Reprinted by permission of Ellen Cassedy.

Laura Cecil for "Moths and Moonshine" by James Reeves from *Complete Poems for Children* (Heinemann), © 1961 James Reeves. Reprinted by permission of the James Reeves Estate.

Nancy Chambers for "Our Panther" by Nancy Chambers from *Stickleback, Stickleback,* originally published by Kestrel Books; Penguin Books, Ltd., © 1977.

Faber and Faber, Ltd., for "Orang-utan" from *Dragonsfire* by Judith Nicholls. Copyright © 1990 by Judith Nicholls. Reprinted by permission of Faber and Faber, Ltd., publishers.

Farrar, Straus and Giroux, Inc., for "Balloons" and "Tent" from *Balloons and Other Poems* by Deborah Chandra. Copyright © 1990 by Deborah Chandra. "Bubble" and "Cricket" from *Rich Lizard and Other Poems* by Deborah Chandra. Text copyright © 1993 by Deborah Chandra. "The Lion" from *Dirty Beasts* by Roald Dahl. Copyright © 1983 by Roald Dahl. "Toaster" from *Laughing Time: Collected Nonsense* by William Jay Smith. Copyright © 1990 by William Jay Smith. "Dinosaurs," "Mosquito," and "Tiger" from *All the Small Poems and Fourteen More* by Valerie Worth. Copyright © 1987, 1994 by Valerie Worth. Reprinted by permission of Farrar, Straus and Giroux, Inc.

Victoria Forrester for "Butterfly Cloth" by Victoria Forrester from *A Latch Against the Wind*. Copyright © 1985 by Victoria Forrester. Reprinted by permission of Victoria Forrester.

Siv Cedering Fox for "If a Bad Dream Comes" from *Blue Horse and Other Night Poems* by Siv Cedering Fox. Copyright © 1979 by Siv Cedering Fox. Reprinted by permission of the author.

Charles Ghigna for "A Poem Is a Little Path" from *Tickle Day: Poems from Father Goose* by Charles Ghigna. Copyright © 1992 by Charles Ghigna. Reprinted by permission of the author.

Greene Bark Press, Inc., for "Tutti Frutti Lovesong" by Mary Grace Dembeck from *Moonsnacks & Assorted Nuts*, published by Greene Bark Press, 1994. Copyright by Mary Grace Dembeck 1994. Reprinted by permission of Greene Bark Press.

Hancock House Publishers for "And My Heart Soars" by Chief Dan George, from *My Heart Soars*. Reprinted by permission of Hancock House Publishers, 1431 Harrison Avenue, Blaine, WA 98230.

Harcourt Brace & Company for "Breaks Free" from *Cactus Poems*, copyright © 1998 by Frank Asch. "The Hawk" from *On the Wing*, copyright © 1996 by Douglas Florian. "The Salmon" from *In the Swim*, copyright © 1997 by Douglas Florian. "Fog" from *Chicago Poems* by Carl Sandburg, copyright 1916 by Holt, Rinehart and Winston and renewed 1944 by Carl Sandburg. "Summer Stars" from *Smoke and Steel* by Carl Sandburg, copyright 1920 by Harcourt Brace & Company and renewed 1948 by Carl Sandburg. "Eating While Reading" from *Canto Familiar*, copyright © 1995 by Gary Soto, reprinted by permission of Harcourt Brace & Company. "What Is the Opposite of Hat?" from *Opposites: Poems and Drawings*, copyright © 1973 by Richard Wilbur. Reprinted by permission of Harcourt Brace & Company.

HarperCollins Publishers, Inc., for "Robert, Who Is Often a Stranger to Himself" by Gwendolyn Brooks. Copyright © 1956 by Gwendolyn Brooks Blakely. "Helicopters" and "Limo" from *Zoomrimes: Poems About Things That Go* by Sylvia Cassedy. Copyright © 1993 by Sylvia Cassedy. "Wolf" from *Words with Wrinkled Knees* by Barbara Juster Esbensen. Copyright © 1986 by Barbara Juster Esbensen. "Homework" by Russell Hoban. Text copyright © 1964, 1972 by Russell Hoban. "Today" from *Hey World, Here I Am!* by Jean Little. Text copyright © 1986 by Jean Little. Used by permission of HarperCollins Publishers. Canadian rights by permission of Kids Can Press Ltd., Toronto, Canada. "For Sale" by Shel Silverstein. Copyright © 1974 by Evil Eye Music, Inc. "Magic" from *Where the Sidewalk Ends* by Shel Silverstein. Copyright © 1974 by Evil Eye Music, Inc. "Magic Landscape" from *Brown Honey in Broomwheat Tea* by Joyce Carol Thomas. Copyright © 1993 by Joyce Carol Thomas. "Building a Skyscraper" and "Autumn Woods" by James S. Tippett from *Crickety Cricket! The Best-Loved Poems of James S. Tippett*. Copyright 1933, copyright renewed © 1973 by Martha K. Tippett. Reprinted by permission of HarperCollins Publishers.

HarperCollins Publishers, Ltd., for "The Secret Place" from *The Ice Cream Store* by Dennis Lee. Published in Canada by HarperCollins Publishers, Ltd., and in the United States by Scholastic, Inc. Copyright © 1991 by Dennis Lee.

David Higham Associates for "The Lion Cub" by Elizabeth Jennings, from *Collected Poems* by Elizabeth Jennings, published by Carcanet. Reprinted by permission of David Higham Associates.

Holiday House for "June," "March," and "September," from *A Child's Calendar* by John Updike. Copyright © 1965, 1999 by John Updike. All rights reserved. Reprinted by permission of Holiday House, Inc.

Henry Holt and Company for "September" from *Everett Anderson's Year* by Lucille Clifton, © 1974 by Lucille Clifton. Reprinted by permission of Henry Holt and Company, Inc. "The Crocodile" from *Creatures Great and Small* by Michael Flanders, © 1964 by Michael Flanders. Reprinted by permission of Henry Holt and Company, Inc. "Blue-Butterfly Day" from *The Poetry of Robert Frost*, edited by Edward Connery Lathem. Copyright 1951 by Robert Frost. Copyright © 1923, © 1969 by Henry Holt and Company. Reprinted by permission of Henry Holt and Company. "That May Morning" from *Is Somewhere Always Far Away?* © 1967 by Leland Jacobs. Reprinted by permission of Henry Holt and Company, Inc. "Doris Skips" from *Alphabet of Girls* by Leland B. Jacobs. Text copyright © 1969 by Leland B. Jacobs. Illustrations copyright © 1994 by Ib Ohlsson. Reprinted by permission of Henry Holt and Company, Ltd.

Houghton Mifflin Co. for "Frizzing" from *Doodle Soup* by John Ciardi. Text copyright © 1985 by Myra J. Ciardi. Reprinted by permission of Houghton Mifflin Co. All rights reserved. "How to Assemble a Toy" from *Mummy Took Cooking Lessons* by John Ciardi. Text copyright © 1990 by Judith C. Ciardi. Reprinted by permission of Houghton Mifflin Co. All rights reserved. "Egg" and "Music Class" from *The Great Frog Race and Other Poems* by Kristine O'Connell George. Text copyright © 1997 by Kristine O'Connell George. Reprinted by permission of Clarion Books/ Houghton Mifflin Co. All rights reserved.

John Johnson Ltd. for "Ears" from *Wry Rhymes for Troublesome Times,* published by Penguin Books Ltd. Copyright © 1983 by Max Fatchen.

Bobbi Katz for "When You Can Read," copyright © 1994 by Bobbi Katz, from *Could We Be Friends? Poems for Pals*, published by Mondo Publishing. Copyright © 1997 by Bobbi Katz.

X. J. and Dorothy M. Kennedy, Ltd., for "Octopus." Copyright © 1999 by X. J. Kennedy. By permission of the author.

Maxine Kumin for "Buses" and "Sneeze" by Maxine Kumin from *No One Writes a Letter to a Snail* (G. P. Putnam's Sons). Copyright © 1962 by Maxine Kumin. Reprinted with permission of the author.

Lee & Low Books, Inc., for "Tickle Tickle" by Dakari Hru. Copyright © 1997 Dakari Hru. From *In Daddy's Arms I Am Tall*. "The Farmer" by Carole Boston Weatherford. Copyright © 1997 by Carole Boston Weatherford. From *In Daddy's Arms I Am Tall*. Reprinted by permission of Lee & Low Books, Inc., 95 Madison Avenue, New York, NY 10016.

Little, Brown and Company for "Shakes and Ladders" from *The Country Mail Is Coming* by Max Fatchen. Copyright © 1987 by Max Fatchen; copyright © 1990 by Catherine O'Neill (illustrations).

Reprinted by permission of Little, Brown and Company. "Big Sister" from *Fathers, Mothers, Sisters, Brothers* by Mary Ann Hoberman. Copyright © 1991 by Mary Ann Hoberman (text); copyright © 1991 by Marilyn Hafner (illustrations). Reprinted by permission of Little, Brown and Company. "Notice" from *One at a Time* by David McCord. Copyright 1952 by David McCord. Reprinted by permission of Little, Brown and Company. "This Is My Rock" from *One at a Time* by David McCord. Copyright 1929 by David McCord. First appeared in *The Saturday Evening Post*. Reprinted by permission of Little, Brown and Company. "The Centipede" from *Custard and Company* by Ogden Nash. Copyright 1935 by Ogden Nash. First appeared in *The Saturday Evening Post*. Reprinted by permission of Little, Brown and Company. "The People Upstairs" from *Custard and Company* by Ogden Nash. Copyright 1949 by Ogden Nash. Reprinted by permission of Little, Brown and Company. "The Sniffle" from *Custard and Company* by Ogden Nash. Copyright 1941 by Ogden Nash. Reprinted by permission of Little, Brown and Company. "Eletelephony" from *Tirra Lirra* by Laura E. Richards. Copyright 1930, 1932 by Laura Richards; copyright © renewed 1960 by Hamilton Richards. Reprinted by permission of Little, Brown and Company.

Liveright Publishing Corporation for "hist whist," copyright 1923, 1951, © 1991 by the Trustees for the E. E. Cummings Trust. Copyright © 1976 by George James Firmage, from *Complete Poems: 1904–1962* by E. E. Cummings, edited by George J. Firmage. Reprinted by permission of Liveright Publishing Corporation.

Gina Maccoby Literary Agency for "Brachiosaurus" from *Yellow Butter, Purple Jelly, Red Jam, Black Bread* by Mary Ann Hoberman. Copyright © 1981 by Mary Ann Hoberman. Reprinted by permission of Gina Maccoby Literary Agency.

Gail Mack for "Hippopotamus" from *The ABC of Bumptious Beasts*. Copyright © 1966 by Gail Kredenser Mack. Reprinted by permission of the author.

McGraw-Hill Book Co., Inc., for "The Sandpiper" from *The Little Whistler* by Robert Frost. Copyright 1949 by Robert Frost and published by Whittlesey House/McGraw-Hill. Reprinted by permission of The McGraw-Hill Companies.

McIntosh and Otis, Inc., for "Mouse Music" from the book *Whispering and Other Things* by Dahlov Ipcar and published by Alfred A. Knopf. Copyright © 1967 by Dahlov Ipcar. Reprinted by permission of McIntosh & Otis, Inc.

Meadowbrook Press for "My Violin" from *Poetry Party* by Bruce Lansky, originally published by Meadowbrook Press. Copyright © 1996 by Bruce Lansky. Reprinted by permission of Meadowbrook Press.

The Edna St. Vincent Millay Society for "Afternoon on a Hill" by Edna St. Vincent Millay. From *Collected Poems*, HarperCollins. Copyright 1917, 1945 by Edna St. Vincent Millay. All rights reserved. Reprinted by permission of Elizabeth Barnett, literary executor.

William Morrow & Company, Inc., for "Chocolate Chocolate" from *Eats* by Arnold Adoff. © 1979 by Arnold Adoff. Reprinted by permission of Lothrop, Lee & Shepard Books, a division of William Morrow & Company, Inc. "Sunflakes" from *Country Pie* by Frank Asch. Copyright © 1979 by Frank Asch. Reprinted by permission of Greenwillow Books, a division of William Morrow & Company, Inc. "Covers" from *Vacation Time* by Nikki Giovanni. Copyright © 1980 by Nikki Giovanni. Reprinted by permission of William Morrow & Company, Inc. "Spinach" and "What You Don't Know About Food" from *Grim and Ghastly Goings-On* by Florence Parry Heide. Copyright © 1992 by Florence Parry Heide. Reprinted by permission of Lothrop, Lee & Shepard Books, a division of William Morrow & Company, Inc. "Loose and Limber" from *Whiskers and Rhymes* by Arnold Lobel. Copyright © 1985 by Arnold Lobel. Reprinted by permission of Greenwillow Books, a division of William Morrow & Company, Inc. "Be Glad Your Nose Is on Your Face" by Jack Prelutsky from *The New Kid on the Block* by Jack Prelutsky. Copyright © 1984 by Jack Prelutsky. Reprinted by permission of Greenwillow Books, a division of William Morrow & Company, Inc. "I Was Walking in a Circle" by Jack Prelutsky from *A Pizza the Size of the Sun* by Jack Prelutsky. Copyright © 1996 by Jack Prelutsky. Reprinted by permission of Greenwillow Books, a division of William Morrow & Company, Inc. "We're Fearless Flying Hotdogs" by Jack Prelutsky from *Something Big Has Been Here* by Jack Prelutsky. Copyright © 1990 by Jack Prelutsky. Reprinted by permission of Greenwillow Books, a division of William Morrow & Company, Inc. "Advice for a Frog" from *Advice for a Frog* by Alice Schertle. Copyright © 1995 by Alice Schertle. Reprinted by permission of Lothrop, Lee & Shepard Books, a division of William Morrow & Company, Inc. "Monopoly" from *Keepers* by Alice Schertle. Copyright © 1996 by Alice Schertle. Reprinted by permission of Lothrop, Lee & Shepard Books, a division of William Morrow & Company, Inc.

Harold Ober Associates for "Cats" from *The Children's Bells* by Eleanor Farjeon. Copyright © 1960 by Eleanor Farjeon. Reprinted by permission of Harold Ober Associates Incorporated. Orchard Books for "Grounded" from *Oh, Grow Up!* by Florence Parry Heide and Roxanne Heide Pierce. Text copyright © 1996 by Florence Parry Heide and Roxanne Heide Pierce. Reprinted by permission of Orchard Books, New York.

Overlook Press for "Ants, Although Admirable, Are Awfully Aggravating" by Walter R. Brooks. From *The Collected Poems of Freddy the Pig* by Walter R. Brooks. Copyright © the Overlook Press. Reprinted by permission of Overlook Press.

Peachtree Publishers, Ltd., for "The Hunter," © 1995 by Ruth Tiller from *Cats Vanish Slowly*. Published by Peachtree Publishers, Ltd. Reprinted by permission of the publisher.

Lydia Pender for "Ditchdiggers" by Lydia Pender from *Morning Magpie—Favourite Verse by Lydia Pender*. First published by Angus & Robertson in Australia, 1984. Used by permission of Lydia Pender.

Penguin Putnam Inc. for "When I Was Lost," from *All Together* by Dorothy Aldis. Copyright 1925–1928, 1934, 1939, 1952, © renewed 1953–1956, 1962 by Dorothy Aldis, © 1967 by Roy E. Porter. Used by permission of G. P. Putnam's Sons, a division of Penguin Putnam Inc. "Noise of Nothing" from *Small Wonders* by Norma Farber. Copyright © 1964, 1968, 1975, 1976, 1978, 1979 by Norma Farber. Used by permission of Coward-McCann, Inc., a division of Penguin Putnam Inc. "At the Library" from *It's Raining Laughter* by Nikki Grimes. Copyright © 1997 by Nikki Grimes. "Genius" from *A Dime a Dozen* by Nikki Grimes. Copyright © 1998 by Nikki Grimes, text. Used by permission of Dial Books for Young Readers, a division of Penguin Putnam Inc. "Red-Winged Blackbird" from *Bird in the Bush* by Grace Taber Hallock. Used by permission of Dutton Children's Books, a division of Penguin Putnam Inc. "Woodpecker" from *Under the North Star* by Ted Hughes. Copyright © 1981 by Ted Hughes. Used by permission of Viking Penguin, a division of Penguin Putnam Inc. "White Cat Winter" from *Once in the Country* by Tony Johnston. Copyright © 1996 by Tony Johnston. Used by permission of G.P. Putnam's Sons, a division of Penguin Putnam Inc. "A Hippopotamusn't" from *A Hippopotamusn't* by J. Patrick Lewis. Copyright © 1990 by J. Patrick Lewis. Used by permission of Dial Books for Young Readers, a division of Penguin Putnam Inc. "The Potato Versus the Pea" from *The Wild Bunch* by Dee Lillegard. Copyright © 1997 by Dee Lillegard. Used by permission of G. P. Putnam's Sons, a division of Penguin Putnam Inc. "The More It Snows" by A. A. Milne, from *The House at Pooh Corner* by A. A. Milne, illustrations by E. H. Shepard. Copyright 1928 by E. P. Dutton, renewed © 1956 by A. A. Milne. Used by permission of Dutton Children's Books, a division of Penguin Putnam Inc.

Jack Prelutsky for "We Are Plooters." Copyright © 1993 by Jack Prelutsky. Used by permission of the author, who controls all rights.

Random House, Inc., for "April Rain Song" and "The Dream Keeper" from *The Dream Keeper and Other Poems* by Langston Hughes. Copyright © 1932 by Alfred A. Knopf, Inc. Copyright renewed 1960 by Langston Hughes. "Alligator Pie" and "Skyscraper" from *Dinosaur Dinner (with a Slice of Alligator Pie)* by Dennis Lee. Compilation copyright © 1974, 1977, 1983, 1991 by Dennis Lee. Reprinted by permission of Alfred A. Knopf, Inc. Canadian rights copyright © 1997 by Dennis Lee. Reprinted by permission of the author. "Fireflies" from *Two-Legged, Four-Legged, No-Legged Rhymes* by J. Patrick Lewis. Copyright © 1991 by J. Patrick Lewis. Reprinted by permission of Alfred A. Knopf, Inc. "Where Are You Now?" from *All Aboard* by Mary Britton Miller. Copyright © 1958 by Pantheon Books, Inc. Reprinted by permission of Pantheon Books, a division of Random House, Inc. Six lines from *On Beyond Zebra!* by Dr. Seuss™ and copyright © 1955 and renewed 1983 by Dr. Seuss Enterprises, L.P. Reprinted by permission of Random House, Inc.

The Estate of James Reeves for "Sky, Sea, Shore" by James Reeves from *Complete Poems for Children* (Heinemann). Copyright © 1961 by James Reeves. Reprinted by permission of the James Reeves Estate.

Marian Reiner for "Trees," the full text of the picture book *Trees* by Harry Behn (Henry Holt & Co.). Copyright © 1949 Harry Behn. Copyright renewed 1977 Alice L. Behn. "Keep a Poem in Your Pocket" from *Something Special* by Beatrice Schenk de Regniers. Copyright © 1958, 1986 Beatrice Schenk de Regniers. "Merry Christmas" from *Feathered Ones and Furry* by Aileen Fisher. Copyright © 1971 by Aileen Fisher. Copyright renewed 1999 by Aileen Fisher. "Tree Climbing" from *Stilts, Somersaults, and Headstands* by Kathleen Fraser. Copyright © 1968 Kathleen Fraser. © renewed 1996 Kathleen Fraser. "Flittermice" and "Sidewalks" from *The Tigers Brought Pink Lemonade* by Patricia Hubbell. Copyright © 1988 by Patricia Hubbell. "Mad Song" from *O Sliver of Liver* by Myra Cohn Livingston. Copyright © 1979 Myra Cohn Livingston (A Margaret K. McElderry Book). "Prayer for Earth" from *Flights of Fancy* by Myra Cohn Livingston (A Margaret K. McElderry Book). Copyright © 1994 by Myra Cohn Livingston. "Reading: Summer" from *Remembering and Other Poems* by Myra Cohn Livingston (A Margaret K. McElderry Book). Copyright © 1989 Myra Cohn Livingston. "Pigeons" from *Rainbow Writing* by Eve Merriam. Copyright © 1976 Eve Merriam. "Weather" from *Catch a Little Rhyme* by Eve Merriam. Copyright © 1966 by Eve Merriam. © renewed 1994 Dee Michel and Guy Michel. "Until I Saw the Sea" from *I Feel the Same Way* by Lillian Moore. Copyright © 1967, 1995 by Lillian Moore. "The Sidewalk Racer" from *The Sidewalk Racer and Other Poems of Sports and Motion* by Lillian Morrison. Copyright © 1965,

1967, 1968, 1977 by Lillian Morrison. © renewed 1993, 1995, 1996 by Lillian Morrison. "Uggle" from *People I'd Like to Keep* by Mary O'Neill. Copyright © 1964 Mary O'Neill. Copyright renewed 1992 Abigail Hagler and Erin Baroni. "Wind Pictures" from *Winds* by Mary O'Neill. Copyright © 1970 Mary O'Neill. Copyright renewed 1998 Abigail Hagler and Erin Baroni. "December Leaves" from *Don't Ever Cross a Crocodile* by Kaye Starbird. Copyright © 1963 Kaye Starbird. © renewed 1991 Kaye Starbird. "New Notebook" from *Flashlight and Other Poems* by Judith Thurman. Copyright © 1976 by Judith Thurman. Reprinted by permission of Marian Reiner for the author.

Denise Ohrenstein Rodgers for "Slicing Salami" by Denise Ohrenstein Rodgers. Copyright © 1998 by Denise Ohrenstein Rodgers. Used by permission of the author, Denise Ohrenstein Rodgers.

Scholastic, Inc., for "Desert Snow" from *This Big Sky* by Pat Mora. Copyright © 1998 by Pat Mora. Reprinted by permission of Scholastic, Inc. "The Click Clacker Machine" by Donna Lugg Pape from *The Book of Foolish Machinery.* Copyright © 1988 by Donna Lugg Pape. Reprinted by permission of Scholastic, Inc.

Simon & Schuster for "No Shop Does the Bird Use" and "Wilderness Rivers." Reprinted with the permission of Simon & Schuster Books for Young Readers, an imprint of Simon & Schuster Children's Publishing Division, from *Summer Green* by Elizabeth Coatsworth. Copyright ©1948 Macmillan Publishing Company; copyright renewed © 1975 Elizabeth Coatsworth Beston. "Some People" and "Something Told the Wild Geese." Reprinted with the permission of Simon & Schuster Books for Young Readers, an imprint of Simon & Schuster Children's Publishing Division, from *Poems* by Rachel Field (Macmillan, New York: 1957). "Undecided." Reprinted with the permission of Atheneum Books for Young Readers, an imprint of Simon & Schuster Children's Publishing Division, from *Ordinary Things* by Ralph Fletcher. Text copyright © 1997 by Ralph Fletcher. "Flashlight" and "My Window Screen." Reprinted with the permission of Margaret K. McElderry Books, an imprint of Simon & Schuster Children's Publishing Division, from *The Forgetful Wishing Well* by X. J. Kennedy. Text copyright © 1985 by X. J. Kennedy. "The Girl Who Makes the Cymbals Bang." Reprinted with the permission of Margaret K. McElderry Books, an imprint of Simon & Schuster Children's Publishing Division, from *The Kite That Braved Old Orchard Beach* by X. J. Kennedy. Text copyright © 1991 by X. J. Kennedy. "Autumn Night Music," "Hawk in the Tree," and "When Whales Exhale" by Constance Levy. Reprinted with the permission of Margaret K. McElderry Books, an imprint of

Simon & Schuster Children's Publishing Division, from *When Whales Exhale and Other Poems* by Constance Levy. Text copyright © 1996 Constance Kling Levy. "The Moon's the North Wind's Cooky." Reprinted with the permission of Simon & Schuster from *The Collected Poems of Vachel Lindsay* by Vachel Lindsay. Copyright 1925 Macmillan Publishing Company; copyright renewed 1953 Elizabeth C. Lindsay. "Channel Changer" and "The Nightnoise Gladiator." Reprinted with permission of Simon & Schuster Books for Young Readers, an imprint of Simon & Schuster Children's Publishing Division, from *Animals That Ought to Be* by Richard Michelson. Text copyright © 1996 Richard Michelson. "Scarecrow Complains." Reprinted with the permission of Atheneum Books for Young Readers, an imprint of Simon & Schuster Children's Publishing Division, from *Adam Mouse's Book of Poems* by Lilian Moore. Text copyright © 1992 Lilian Moore. "Sea Song." Reprinted with the permission of Atheneum Books for Young Readers, an imprint of Simon & Schuster Children's Publishing Division, from *Poems Have Roots* by Lilian Moore. Text copyright © 1997 Lilian Moore. "You Never Hear the Garden Grow." Reprinted with the permission of Atheneum Books for Young Readers, an imprint of Simon & Schuster Children's Publishing Division, from *I'll Meet You at the Cucumbers* by Lilian Moore. Text copyright © 1988 Lilian Moore. "april is a dog's dream" and "Turtle in July." Reprinted with the permission of Atheneum Books for Young Readers, an imprint of Simon & Schuster Children's Publishing Division, from *Turtle in July* by Marilyn Singer. Text copyright © 1989 Marilyn Singer. "Flags." Reprinted with the permission of Simon & Schuster Books for Young Readers, an imprint of Simon & Schuster Children's Publishing Division, from *A Moon for Seasons* by Ann Turner. Text copyright © 1994 Ann Turner. "Learning" and "Stanley the Fierce" by Judith Viorst. Reprinted with the permission of Atheneum Books for Young Readers, an imprint of Simon & Schuster Children's Publishing Division, from *If I Were in Charge of the World and Other Worries* by Judith Viorst. Text copyright © 1981 Judith Viorst. "Noodles." Reprinted with the permission of Margaret K. McElderry Books, an imprint of Simon & Schuster Children's Publishing Division from *Good Luck Gold and Other Poems* by Janet S. Wong. Copyright © 1994 Janet S. Wong.

Zilpha Keatly Snyder for "Poem to Mud" from *Today Is Saturday* by Zilpha Keatly Snyder. Copyright © 1969 by Zilpha Keatly Snyder. Reprinted by permission of Zilpha Keatly Snyder.

The Society of Authors for "All But Blind," "The Snowflake," and "Tired Tim" by Walter de la Mare. Reprinted by permission of The Literary Trustees of Walter de la Mare, and the Society

of Authors as their representative.

Scott Treimel New York for "Me" and "Rules" from *Alexander Soames: His Poems* by Karla Kuskin. Copyright © 1962, 1980 by Karla Kuskin. "Spring" from *In the Middle of the Trees* by Karla Kuskin. Copyright © 1959, renewed 1986 by Karla Kuskin. "Autumn" and "River in Winter" from *River in Winter* by Charlotte Zolotow. Copyright © 1970 by Charlotte Zolotow. Reprinted by permission of Scott Treimel New York.

United Methodist Publishing House for "Thanksgiving" by Ivy O. Eastwick from *Cherry Stones! Garden Swings! Poems* by Ivy O. Eastwick, illustrated by Robert A. Jones. Copyright © 1962 by Abingdon Press. Used by permission.

Valen Associates for "I Can Fly" and "Night Sounds" from *At the Top of My Voice and Other Poems* by Felice Holman. Charles Scribner's Sons © 1970. Used by permission of Felice Holman. "Tuning Up" from *I Hear You Smiling and Other Poems* by Felice Holman. Charles Scribner's Sons ©1973. Reprinted by permission of Felice Holman.

Colin West for "Norman Norton's Nostrils" from *The Best of West* (Hutchinson, 1990). Copyright © 1982 by Colin West. "Rolling Down a Hill" from *The Best of West* (Hutchinson, 1990). Copyright © 1988 by Colin West. Reprinted by permission of the author.

Rhoda Weyr Agency for "A Bat Is Born" from the book *The Bat-Poet* by Randall Jarrell, published by Michael di Capua Books/ HarperCollins Publishers. © 1963, 1965 by Randall Jarrell. Permission granted by Rhoda Weyr Agency, NY.

Albert Whitman & Company for "The Nest" from *The Dreams of Hummingbirds: Poems from Nature* by Mary Ann Coleman. Copyright © 1993 by Mary Ann Coleman. Reprinted by permission of Albert Whitman & Company.